205

D1315422

Move
HOUSE

Move
HOUSE

Sean Topham

Prestel Munich · Berlin · London · New York

Contents

Nomad´s Land

1234

Arthur Rackham, The Open Road, illustration from
Kenneth Grahame's The Wind in the Willows.

Shamanistic altar in yurt, Mongolia.

Maybe I watch too much TV but there have been moments when I was really taken by the idea of living in the back of a van. Weekly doses of TV shows such as *Scooby Doo* and *The A-Team* made life on the road seem full of excitement and adventure. Each week meant a new town, new friends and a mystery to solve or wrong-doer to put right. The A-Team, four renegade commandos on the run from the military police, evaded the authorities with the aid of a sleek black custom van. The vehicle, a 1983 GMC G-Series with modifications by Universal Studios' prop department, was hardly a living space but it represented home to the heroes of the show. Its interior featured bespoke bucket seats, shag carpet, numerous electronic devices, and a cache of arms. On the outside it was decorated with a rear spoiler, wide wheels, and red go-faster stripe. An array of fog lights and a low-hanging sun visor gave it a mean look that reflected the attitude of its occupants.

Shows such as *The A-Team* follow in a long line of fictional works that romanticize the traveling lifestyle. Westerns, for example, often celebrate lone gun slingers who ride into a town and solve all its problems—or maybe create a whole lot more. Authors such as Charles Dickens in *The Old Curiosity Shop* and Kenneth Grahame in *The Wind in the Willows*, in their descriptions of caravans, demonstrate a great fondness for traveling folk and their way of life. "There's real life for you," says Mr. Toad in *The Wind in the Willows*, referring to a canary yellow Gypsy caravan, "Here today, up and off to somewhere else tomorrow!" Toad's enthusiasm for mobile dwellings was shared also by countless bored teenagers looking to break free from the family home. A beaten-up van with a mattress thrown on the floor became the staple live-in vehicle for

numerous youth culture movements in the second half of the 20th century. For surfers it was the "woody", for flower-power kids the Volkswagen Camper, and where would the British punk scene have been without the Ford Transit van? Such vehicles represent the equivalent of a first home and a personal space away from the prying eyes of parents. The current crop of mobile dwellings created by architects, artists, self-builders, and designers share the same motivations that persuade a bored kid to escape into a van. They embody rebellion and dissatisfaction, flamboyant showing off, a need for privacy and yet a contrasting desire to socialize and meet people.

Unfortunately not all people from static civilizations show as much affection for portable dwellings as thrill-seeking teenagers and Mr. Toad. Throughout history travelers of all kinds have been subject to routine insults and abuse. The same can be said for the dwellings they call home. Mobile dwellings have a bad reputation. The term "trailer-park trash" is used commonly to refer to a person—usually from the southern states of the USA—who lacks class, intelligence, and decorum. It assumes that a person living in a mobile home is somehow inferior to a person who occupies a static, site-built house. It is by no means a new idea. Back in the 5th century BC the city-dwelling Athenians considered the nomadic Scythians, their neighbors on the Crimean steppe, in much the same way. The belief that settled civilizations were superior to mobile tribes persisted through much of European and then North American history and gave rise to the image of the nomad as a primitive savage. As a consequence, the solid stone buildings of past empires have for centuries been celebrated by historians as great works of architecture whereas the portable structures used by nomads, until recently,

Women and children in a yurt camp, Mongolia.

Yurt/ger in the Altai Mountains.

remain largely ignored. The European nations may have preferred permanent monumental structures but they relied heavily on portable dwellings to build and maintain their enormous empires. The Manning Portable Colonial Cottage for Emigrants and the Hersteller Iron Cottage for Emigrants were among several portable housing options for British and European people relocating to the colonies in the mid-19th century.

Even today, the modern mobile home is rarely considered for the quality of its design. The typical trailer home, or manufactured home as it has come to be known, has a laughable reputation in many design circles. It is considered ugly and cumbersome, yet such dwellings are immensely popular and represent around a quarter of all housing in the USA. The motor home and travel trailer or caravan are similarly enjoyed by millions of people around the world, but remain ignored or ridiculed as examples of design. By sharp contrast, recent years have seen more and more architects, designers, and artists fall in love with the freedom offered by the portable dwelling. These latest additions to the story of the mobile dwelling make up a large proportion of the projects featured in this book and no matter how slick or how radical some of the examples may seem, it is worth remembering that they owe a great debt to the much maligned trailer home.

Mobile homes from other cultures are a far cry from the boxes on wheels that typically spring to mind in the USA and Europe. The yurt, for example, is an exceptionally flexible house type that has served pastoral nomads including the Kazakhs, Uzbeks, Kyrgyz, Turkmenians and various Mongol tribes for centuries. It was developed to cope with the harsh conditions of the Eurasian

steppe, a vast area of grassy plain stretching over 3,000 kilometers from the Caspian Sea to central Mongolia. Essentially a circular dwelling, the yurt is made with wooden, lattice frame walls and across these are laid arc-shaped or sometimes straight wooden poles that form the roof. Once secured, the wooden frame is coated with typically woolen but in some circumstances reed mats that are strapped in place with rope or webbing bands. A smoke hole is left open in the center of the roof and the door can be made with a rolled felt mat, a solid carved wooden panel, or a pair of wooden doors attached by leather hinges.

The threshold between the exterior and interior of a yurt is of symbolic importance and, once inside, one must always follow a clockwise path. The interior is divided strictly into quadrants around a central hearth. An altar sits in the quadrant opposite the entrance and space here is also reserved for honored guests. To the left of the doorway is the family head's quadrant and to the right is the women's and children's area. If the family has a herder he occupies the space immediately to the right of the door alongside the cooking utensils. Saddles and weapons are placed immediately to the left of the door and other items such as rugs, bedding, and clothes are stored around the perimeter.

The thick woolen waistcoats traditionally worn by the nomadic herdsmen are tied around their bodies in a manner similar to the wrapping of the felt mats around the framework of the home. The limited resources available on the harsh steppe mean that the covering for the home and clothing for the body are often created from the same fabric. This creates a close relationship between the two and clothing effectively becomes an offshoot of the home (and

Medicine Man Little Big Mouth in front of his tipi.

Tent stands at Bedouin camp site.

perhaps vice versa). The fabrics used share the same qualities and offer similar levels of protection against the elements. The same can be said of the clothing and dwellings employed by nomadic tribes of Native Americans who occupied the North American plains. Their garments and the fabric of their homes were traditionally made from buffalo hide, one of the few materials in abundance. The yurt and the tipi are both skin-on-frame constructions designed to be easily erected, dismantled, and transported. The tipi's conical shape is formed by a framework of long wooden poles tied near the top and spread out to create an almost circular plan on the ground. The wooden skeleton is covered with a semicircular sheet made from buffalo hides, which cloaks the frame and is fastened together with pegs. The entrance always faces east and is typically an oval-shaped hole with a flap of buffalo hide for a door.

The black tent used by the bedouin nomads who occupy the deserts of the Middle East and North Africa is a further example of a textile dwelling. It differs from the yurt and tipi because it uses tension as a means of support rather than a rigid structural frame. Bedouin tents are created from rectangular strips of woven goat hair and wool cloth supported on wooden poles and secured by guy ropes. A typical tent will have twelve or thirteen support poles: ten form the perimeter and two or three support the roof across its middle. The central poles are slightly taller than those in the walls and the space between poles tends to vary between three and four meters. The front wall or "face" of the home is removed during the day unless the weather is bad or there is a need for privacy. The other walls can also be lifted to aid ventilation in the desert heat and the natural properties of the wool cause it to swell in wet weather, which makes

it waterproof. Simpler fabric is used around the tent edges as this is subject to greater wear and can be replaced more regularly than the panels of the roof.

Like the yurt, the interior of the Bedouin tent is divided strictly between the family head and his wife and children. A curtain suspended from the wooden poles provides a physical barrier between the public and private areas of the home. The public area is the male domain where guests are received and entertained. Food preparation and childcare occurs on the private, female side of the divide, which is also where the whole family sleeps. The size of the two halves of the tent depends on the number and the needs of its inhabitants. A large family needs a larger area for sleeping, storage, and cooking, while a sheikh needs more space to receive guests and conduct business.

The black tent, the yurt, and the tipi are formidable dwellings ideally suited to the hostile environments from which they offer shelter. All can be packed down for transit and erected or dismantled quickly and with ease, but contradict sharply the notion that mobile dwellings offer freedom. The interior layout of each dwelling is governed by strict codes that help maintain a sense of history and tradition. Pastoral nomads do not wander aimlessly across the plains and deserts, but follow patterns directed by the grazing habits of their herds.

Animals, in this case horses, also have a major impact on the dwellings and movements of the nomadic Roma people or Gypsies. Horse-trading has traditionally provided the backbone of the Roma economy and a network of large fairs still exists as essential gathering places for Gypsy travelers. Romany people in Europe traditionally

lived in demountable structures known as benders before switching gradually to the horse-drawn Gypsy wagon or vardo in the 19th century. Benders were erected by covering a hoop-shaped framework of bent sapling wood with blankets or felt. The vardo slowly replaced the bender as road surfaces improved, but many Roma continued to use the shelters as additional accommodation. The most common type of Gypsy wagon was the bowtop, which had a fabric roof stretched over a frame of rounded, wooden bows mounted on a four-wheeled cart or dray. The design is very light and resembles the prairie schooners used by settlers traversing the American plains.

Contrasting sharply with the modest, lightweight Gypsy wagon was the ornate showman's living van. These occasionally extravagant affairs are the direct ancestors of today's motor homes and recreational vehicles. A Venetian showman named Antoine Franconi is thought to have been one of the first people to design and live in what we would now recognize as a caravan or recreational trailer. His show traveled around Europe in the early 19th century and his mobile home was known as a "voiture nomad." The living van of a showman had a distinct appearance that reflected the ostentatious nature of his art and announced his arrival in town. An English showman named Walter Murphy commissioned a van from a firm called Orton & Spooner that included electric lights and heaters and was over nine meters long. The firm was well known for its ornate carving and woodwork, which is demonstrated in the mahogany finish of Murphy's van. These early homes on wheels were a totally new house type and were usually created in close collaboration between an owner and a craftsman. The result was a unique reflection of the owner's distinct character and personal concept of home.

The earliest recreational trailers were based on the living vans used by traveling showmen and became very fashionable among the European middle classes during the early 20th century. The Caravan Club of Great Britain and Ireland was formed in June 1907 by the writer and barrister J. Harris Stone and ten other enthusiasts. The Vice-President of the Club was the elderly Dr. W. Gordon Stables, one of the first people to take to the road for leisure purposes. His pleasure caravan was called the Wanderer and in 1886 he wrote about his travels in the book *The Cruise of the Land Yacht Wanderer*. Dr. Stables's van was designed to be pulled by two horses and measured 6 meters in length by 3.35 meters high. The interior was divided into two rooms: a saloon area that transformed into sleeping quarters and a combined kitchen and washroom at the rear. A coachman and a valet accompanied Dr. Stables on his travels along with a dog and a parrot. The Wanderer was built largely with solid mahogany and sometimes proved too heavy for the horses, especially when climbing steep hills.

Dr. Stables achieved certain notoriety from his travels in the Wanderer and it was not long before other wealthy ladies and gentlemen were engaged in the new hobby. The advent of improved road surfaces, motor driven homes and travel trailers saw the popularity of van living as a leisure pursuit increase even further. Early caravan enthusiasts tended to fall into two camps: those who did not want to sacrifice the luxuries of home while on the move and those who were willing to forgo comfort in favor of increased mobility. The former used mobile dwellings as capsules that preserved their sense of propriety while on the move. Dr. Stables was positioned firmly in this camp and distanced himself from traditional travelers.

1932 Silver Cloud Model Airstream. This is the first trailer that Airstream ever produced. It was designed in 1931 and built in the California plant in 1932.

Most innovations in the design and construction of the new recreational vehicles were made by the people who used them. These houses on wheels were a completely new proposition for wheelwrights and coach builders, whose craft developed at a time when sturdy carriages were required to cope with the terrible road surfaces of the 19th century. The new and increasing demand for lightweight touring boxes led to many experiments by amateur builders that shaped the leisure caravan as it is today. Members of the Caravan Club compared new concepts at annual meetings, which developed into forums for the exchange of ideas. Travel trailers and motor homes in the 1920s became lighter, smaller, and more aerodynamic. The popularity of motoring holidays continued to grow, especially in the United States where sales of commercially manufactured recreational vehicles increased at a rapid rate.

Arthur Sherman, a Minnesota bacteriologist, designed and mass-produced an inexpensive, plywood caravan named the Covered Wagon in 1929. He was inspired to do so after struggling to erect a tent in the rain on an earlier family vacation. Sherman started making the trailers in his garage, but by 1936 he was one of the biggest manufacturers of travel trailers in the USA. Better vehicles and a network of reliable highways enabled the trend for motoring holidays to boom. Trailer tourism became such a popular pastime that by 1936 several cities in the warmer southern states began introducing laws that limited the number of places where campers could park and the length of time they could stay. Those making the long journey from the northern to southern states would regularly stock up on canned provisions and this resulted in them being dubbed "tin can tourists."

It was not just innovations in the automotive industry that propelled the trend for the recreational trailer. Aircraft design also had an impact, and in 1936 Wally Byam unveiled the Clipper, the first in a long line of classic Airstream trailers. The Clipper was a revolutionary design and featured the characteristic rivet-fastened aluminum body and bullet-shaped nose that Airstream is now famous for. Inside were four bunks, a tubular metal dinette, and a separate fitted kitchen. Other selling points included advanced systems for heating, electricity, and ventilation, and although the Clipper was an expensive product for its time, Airstream struggled to meet all the orders it received. Nowadays there are plenty of commercially manufactured recreational vehicles on the market, ranging from the modest trailer-tent to the spacious A-class motor home, but a few dedicated enthusiasts still prefer to design and build their own.

Seasonal and itinerant workers in the USA began adopting recreational trailers as temporary homes during the Depression of the 1930s. Then, during World War Two, the need to build instant communities around munitions factories, shipyards, and other manufacturing works led to the rapid development of trailer parks. Such parks continued to grow as soldiers wanting to set up home returned from overseas and large, all-weather travel trailers with electricity and heating, such as the 1946 Spartan, were used as models for year-round trailer homes. These earlier trailer homes were streamlined and dynamic; they looked like they were intended to move —and at speed. It was also around this time that R. Buckminster Fuller unveiled his cylindrical Wichita House (1947). The dynamic, aluminum home resembled a yurt for the atomic age but never made it into full-scale production. Another remarkable innovation

1936 Airstream Clipper.

Advertisement for the 1946 Spartan Manor.

1963 Magnolia Leisurama (triple-wide). This is the first model that Magnolia produced. These homes were continually produced until 1980.

to appear during this period was the introduction of paper houses. These were created after the US War Production board asked the Institute of Paper Chemistry to develop a cheap, portable house that could be mass produced and used as emergency shelter. Later paper dwellings include the Plydom, designed in the 1960s by Hirsham and van der Ryn to house itinerant farm workers in California. The Plydom had a concertina-like structural shell that gave it added strength and folded down for easy storage and transportation.

By the late 1960s manufacturers of trailer homes started to make them roomier and introduced double- and then triple-wides (two or three separate trailers fastened together to create a single, larger home). Mobile homes no longer looked mobile and more and more resembled a traditional site-built home. "Modular" or "manu-factured" is the preferred term for mobile homes today and this is quite appropriate because the only move made by the majority of them is from the factory to the initial resting site. The most dynamic-looking portable homes arrived just as the conventional trailer homes began settling down to a life of immobility. Futuristic pods made of plastic and resembling flying saucers were marketed as space-age ski cabins and hi-tech holiday retreats. Jean Maneval's Six Shell Bubble House (1968) signaled the arrival of a new breed of portable home. As its name suggests, the dwelling consisted of six separate self-supporting shells that were fastened and sealed together with a series of flexible joints. The outer casing was fabri-cated from reinforced polyester plastic and the interior included its own range of furniture designed to fit the curves of each shell. Once dismantled, the house fitted on to the back of a truck for delivery to a new location, where it could be erected with relative ease.

However, the Six Shell Bubble House was only in commercial pro-duction from 1968 to 1970 and only about thirty were ever made. Most of those were used as accommodation units at an experimental holiday resort in the village of Gripp in the Spanish Pyrenees.

An equally short-lived plastic house was designed by Finnish architect Matti Suuronen. His Futuro House (1968) was first devel-oped as a ski cabin that could be delivered to remote mountain locations, either in one piece by helicopter, or transported by truck and assembled on site. Futuro went into production in 1968 and its flying-saucer-like exterior was formed by sixteen separate panels, which were fastened together on the turn-key principle. The house received an enormous amount of publicity on its launch but failed to live up to its billing as the home of tomorrow.

Space travel itself resulted in the development of pressurized, fully portable environments that allowed astronauts and cosmonauts to endure lengthy stays outside the earth's atmosphere. A space station is a mobile dwelling with all the facilities and life support systems that its crew needs to survive in the severe conditions of space. It is easy to appreciate a space station as a mobile home: it is a container with solid exterior walls and an interior divided into zones for specific tasks, much the same as a regular earth-bound yurt or trailer. A space suit or extravehicular mobility unit (EMU) might be thought of more readily as clothing, but it offers all the life support systems and protection of a space station in a condensed and incred-ibly flexible package. It is a fully mobile environment that allows a per-son to function for a limited period of time away from a spacecraft.

The battle to reach the moon in the 1960s saw mobility and mobile dwellings become a prime concern for an international

Advertisement for the 1956 Richardson
Bi-Level Trailer.

Jean Maneval, Six-shell Bubble House, 1968.

network of architects. Radical groups including Archigram in England, Utopie in France, Haus-Rucker-Co. in Austria, and the Metabolists in Japan envisioned the city of the future as a dynamic entity in constant change. Mobile dwelling units, inspired by the space age and the rapid onset of the throwaway consumer culture, were central to these visions. Permanent buildings would become redundant and give way to flexible structures better able to cope with the demands of a society in flux. The groups devised inflatable capsules, plastic pods, and "plug-in" apartments capable of continuous transformation to new situations. Japanese architect Kisho Kurokawa was a key figure in the Metabolist movement and completed the Nagakin Capsule Tower in Tokyo in 1972. The apartment block functions in a similar manner to a trailer park, only vertically. The individual capsules plug-in to a core structure that supplies the essential systems such as energy, water, and sanitation. The central core is a permanent structure, but the apartments were designed to be removed, exchanged, and transported to other locations.

While these architects looked to the future for ideas to shape the mobile home, others looked to the past. The Romany community in particular provided a massive inspiration for groups of hippies in the 1960s who wanted to establish a way of life free from the trappings of mainstream society. Elements of the counter culture hit the road and established a series of festivals as forums to express creativity and share information. Many took up residence in converted vehicles such as delivery vans and old school buses. A spirit of improvization reigned in these homes on wheels. Some were psychedelic eyesores covered in swirls of day-glo paint and random slogans, while others were clad in wood and adopted the more

folklike appearance of a prairie home on a roller skate. Some of the most unusual examples were created by welding the shell of a camper van onto the top of a bus to form a DIY double-decker. The hippies gave redundant vehicles a whole new lease of life and would often fit them with other found objects such as discarded furniture and old stoves. The development of these mobile homes followed a similar pattern to the evolution of the first leisure caravans. They were not commercially available products. The campers who built the first travel trailers experimented with different materials and designs and shared their innovations with others. The hippies did the same. The popularity of the alternative lifestyle grew in the 1970s and books offering advice and inspiration were published, such as *Roll Your Own* by Jodi Pallidini and Beverly Dubin and *Rolling Homes* by Jane Lidz.

One of the most famous "rolling homes" belonged to Ken Kesey, author of *One Flew Over the Cuckoo's Nest*, and a group of friends calling themselves the Merry Pranksters. The vehicle started out as a 1939 International Harvester school bus but was transformed into a psychedelic shack on wheels for a voyage from California to New York and back in the summer of 1964. The bus was given the name "Furthur" (sometimes written as "Further") for good luck by Prankster Roy Sebern, who was among the first people to paint it. Ken Babbs, another Merry Prankster, described Furthur shortly before its maiden trip: "The rig seemingly has the dimensions of an aircraft carrier. Three tiers of bunks line the sides of the back third. The mid third consists of a dining suite bolted to the floor, along with a complete kitchen." Furthur was both a mobile home and a performance piece. Its noisy coloring and the reputation of its passengers

Matti Suuronen, Futuro House, Finland, 1968.

drew plenty of attention from the press and public alike as it meandered across America.

Bus dwelling also proved popular in Britain, where the new traveling community continued to grow through the late 1970s and into the 1980s. The improvised mobile homes were again created from buses, vans, and other vehicles that could be obtained cheaply but still satisfied motor-transport regulations. They varied in layout and style but many seemed to celebrate the new-found freedom offered by life away from the recession-hit inner cities. A circuit of free festivals provided the foundation of the traveler economy. The growing popularity of these events led to many confrontations with the authorities. One of the biggest clashes erupted near Stonehenge in June 1985 after a massive convoy of travelers was ambushed by the police. It represented a new and violent era of intolerance by the government toward the traveling community. New Acts of Parliament were introduced to curb the freedoms of the traveling community and life on the road became increasingly harsh. The change of mood was reflected in the vehicles the travelers used as homes. They became more discreet with little or no exterior decoration so as to appear indistinguishable from a normal passenger coach. This stealth look was also adopted by the mobile sound systems that appeared on what was left of the free festival circuit in the late 1980s. DJ collectives such as DiY and Spiral Tribe took to the road to play house and techno music at impromptu parties across Britain. Some of the vehicles used by the traveling sound systems were adorned with camouflage patterns and military insignia that symbolized the escalation in tension between them and the authorities.

The free festival scene of the 1980s and 1990s shaped dance music culture as it exists today and provided the inspiration for other art and music festivals such as the Burning Man event, held annually in the Nevada desert. Burning Man is a temporary town where thousands descend to party for a week and then vanish without leaving a trace. The festival is home to all manner of temporary shelters from geodesic domes to straw-bale shacks, and attracts an equally diverse crowd. Every person who attends the festival must contribute to it in some way and in doing so becomes a participant in the proceedings rather than an observer. The festival is held deep in the desert far from any supplies of water or power, so everything needed has to be transported to the site.

For those of us living in settled urban centers it is largely through leisure or working vehicles that we experience life on the move for ourselves. Workers in the fishing and water transport communities, truck drivers, and corporate executives all rely on mobile dwellings that also function as workplaces. For the long-distance haulage driver, the cab of a truck represents a home away from home and for a few it functions as a full-time residence. The roadside diner, CB radio, email, and mobile telephones all enable truckers to maintain a strong sense of community even though individual drivers may spend days in isolation on the road. Fully equipped bathrooms and kitchens, satellite TV, wood paneling, curtains, rugs, and floor tiles all add touches of domesticity and help create a sense of home on the move. Comparable to the trucker's cab is the private aircraft equipped to operate as a combined home and office. Travel schedules for those researching emerging markets can be particularly grueling and such live/work spaces in the sky are essential for the executive

Kisho Kurokawa's Nagakin Capsule Tower, 1972.

NASA's Extravehicular Mobility Suit.

who needs to be everywhere at once. The interiors of private aircraft, however, often lack the small hints of domesticity that can often be found in a trucker's cab. They are not inhabited for such lengthy periods of time but a few wealthy owners have managed to add personal touches and incorporate their own identity into the interiors of their aircraft. One example is Hugh Hefner, the *Playboy* publisher, who in 1970 unveiled his very own jet-powered bachelor pad. The exterior of the aircraft, a McDonnell Douglas DC-9 dubbed the "Big Bunny", had a glossy black finish while the famous Playboy bunny motif was used as the insignia on the tail fin. The luxurious interior featured a fur-covered bed with a cushioned black leather headboard and beside it a modern black leather armchair. The interior wall of the airplane was sculpted over the bed and incorporated an instrument panel with controls for the on-board audio and video entertainment systems. Partitions of dark wood divided the bedroom from the remainder of the orange upholstered cabin. The pursuit of pleasure was obviously a major influence on the design of the "Big Bunny" and it balanced the functions of a work place and relaxing retreat in a tightly organized capsule.

As this short history has shown, the big attraction of the mobile dwelling is that it can belong to us all. The mobile home does not have a history associated with any single nation, race, or class. The modern mobile home—like the dwellings used by traditional nomadic tribes—was designed and developed by the people who use it. This book is a celebration of contemporary interpretations of the mobile dwelling. The examples range from recreational vehicles for retirees to clandestine dwellings for squatters. Some

are practical and others theoretical, yet all point to a desire among a wide variety of people for a house that can be relocated when the need arises. It is the notion that the portable dwelling belongs to us all that has prompted so many people from a variety of backgrounds to define their own unique vision of what a mobile home can be, which is why I felt it essential to include projects by self-builders alongside the work of architects, fashion and product designers, artists and commercial manufacturers. Younger architects especially seem keen to fashion mobile dwelling units, with varying degrees of success. This could be a reflection on the impracticality of student life, which can often involve multiple changes of address in a relatively short time period. For students living away from home—especially those studying overseas—the mobile dwelling represents a desire for a familiar space in a new and unfamiliar environment.

The book has been divided into four chapters that loosely bring together some of the key attractions of the mobile home. Few people would like to think of their homes as weapons but the dwellings grouped together in the opening chapter, titled "Fight the Power" can be seen as just that. These dwellings employ mobility as a way of skirting around building codes and of offering an alternative way of life away from mainstream society. "Flexible Friends" looks at contemporary interpretations of some of the oldest structures to be created by man. Nomadic dwellings such as the tipi, the yurt, and the Bedouin tent demonstrate a close relationship between clothing and shelter. This chapter includes clothes that transform into basic dwellings alongside folding structures that can easily be packed away for transportation. "Taking the Trailer Park Uptown"

Further, the Merry Pranksters' Bus.

Live to Ride / Ride to Live, a customized Peterbilt 379 at the 1999 Reno Truckers' Jamboree, Reno, Nevada.

does exactly that. All too often architects come up with a really novel design for a mobile home, but then go and spoil it by describing it as an "affordable" option for those unable to purchase a "proper" house. The dwellings in this chapter demonstrate that not all mobile homes are cheap alternatives to a permanent property. "Oasis" acknowledges that one of the more appealing aspects of the mobile home lies in its capacity to demand social interaction. Temporary communities, formed when like-minded travelers converge on a single location, provide an oasis of nourishment for the lonely nomad, while also aiding innovation in the design of all kinds of mobile dwellings. The mobile homes in this chapter are able to transform from private to public spaces when the need arises, and form a small part of the numerous roaming networks that reach across continents and right around the world.

All the examples included contribute to the ongoing development of the mobile dwelling. Many are dedicated to the creation of a shelter suited to a specific situation where a permanent dwelling would prove impractical. Some show how a mobile dwelling can be either an intimate space that offers protection or a skeletal shelter that plunges its occupant into new and unexpected situations. All offer fascinating insights into alternative ways of living and defining what we call home.

Fight the Power

1234

Michael Jantzen's rural upbringing has had a major influence on his work as an artist. Volatile thunderstorms regularly knocked out electricity supplies in his native state of Illinois and made him realize he couldn't always rely on the national grid to power his home. Self-sufficiency is a prime concern of Jantzen's work and this is demonstrated perfectly by Autonomous Dwelling (p. 24), which he designed and built with Ted Bakewell, a property developer who made the Dwelling his home for over five years.

Bakewell took care of the engineering, power and plumbing of Autonomous Dwelling while Jantzen concentrated on achieving a very tight and highly functional design for the limited amount of space. The home may resemble a futuristic space capsule but its distinctive shape owes more to farmyard outbuildings than the space shuttle. The two quarter-spheres at either end of the Autonomous Dwelling are two halves of a metallic dome used to cap the tops of grain silos.

One of Jantzen's aims with his dwellings is to create "building systems that have the freedom to generate new and unexpected forms." Jantzen admits he is "pretty bored" with conventional domestic architecture and this has pushed him to experiment with new construction technologies. The striking appearance of his M House is derived directly from its modular construction. The basic building blocks are cubic frames made with tubular steel. Attached to these frames are insulated panels of concrete composite that form the walls of the interior spaces. Some panels contain windows or doors and others are used as platforms or decks, creating a mixture of interior and exterior spaces within the boundary of the dwelling. Further adjustable panels are attached to the frames with hinges to provide shelter from sun, wind, or rain. The M House pictured is made of seven cubic frames and rests on a series of telescopic legs.

Jantzen has for the most part concentrated his efforts on individual dwellings but Home-SCAPE (p. 25) is a proposal to create a small community of homes. The construction technique is based on structural insulated panels that can be cut and joined to create all manner of complex forms. New modules can be added to the central unit as the family occupying it grows. That same module can then form the basis of a new home when a family member decides it's time to move on.

M House rests on a network of telescopic legs that can be adapted to a range of surfaces. Shaded areas inside the dwelling are created inside by adjusting the numerous hinged panels. The whole house can be dismantled and reconfigured in a matter of days.

Michael Jantzen, USA
M House, 1999

Michael Jantzen, USA

Autonomous Dwelling, 1980 (in collaboration with Ted Bakewell)
Home-SCAPE, 2000

Autonomous Dwelling was designed and built for a real estate developer who spent much of his time living on construction sites which were not yet hooked up to the grid. The futuristic mobile home is completely self-sufficient and generates its power from the sun and wind.

The curved, irregular forms of Home-SCAPE result from the self-supporting foam panels used as the basis of its construction. A variety of finishes can be applied to the panels such as wood veneer on the walls and metal on the roof.

Sean Godsell, Australia

Park Bench House, 2002

While private firms and city legislators try their best to sweep away homeless people from public spaces, Sean Godsell's controversial Park Bench House appears to encourage sleeping rough. The architect has stripped away the arm rests and other barriers that prevent people from bedding down on public benches and has added a woven wire bed and even an automatic night light to make this street furniture more accommodating.

For sitting, the device resembles an oversized bench but when needed for sleeping the seat lifts and can be secured to form a roof over the person inside. A light glows underneath to signal to others that the bed is occupied and, perhaps more importantly, serves as a very visible reminder that homelessness is a problem that cannot be solved by tucking it out of sight.

Park Bench House provoked a mixed response when Godsell presented it to the city authorities of Melbourne and Port Talbot in Southern Australia. A welfare officer writing in *The Age*, Melbourne's daily newspaper, criticized it as a "Band-Aid measure" and a "ruthlessly pragmatic response to inner-city homelessness." He also pointed out that the estimated cost of a single bench (AUS$2,700) was enough to pay the rent in a public housing apartment for a whole year. Other questions ranged from who would move people on in the morning, to what happens when one person wants to sleep and others want to sit?

Despite all the questions raised by Park Bench House the architect has illuminated a concern that the homeless are increasingly excluded from public spaces. Godsell accepts that some members of the homeless community prefer sleeping on the street to staying at a municipal shelter. The Park Bench House provides a space in the city for rough sleepers, and suggests that merely clearing those deemed "illegal campers" from public parks and squares will not solve the problems associated with homelessness.

By day it's a bench, by night a bed. Simply lift up the seat and climb inside. Park Bench House is a rudimentary shelter for people who sleep rough in public spaces. The small solar panel powers a light that glows to show the bed is occupied.

Gregor Passens, Germany
Caterpillar, 1999

Caterpillar is a house made of metal that has been tipped over to resemble a tank. A network of ventilation piping holds the house together and points out from the pitched roof to suggest both a chimney and the barrel of a gun. The title has associations with both the tracks tanks and other heavy vehicles are driven on, and the worm-like larva that metamorphoses into a moth or butterfly. Passens's sculpture transforms a symbol of home into a symbol of war. It has a skin of corrugated metal sheets that is hard and tough like armor plating, but it has no firepower like a real tank. In times of conflict tanks are used to conquer and defend territories. The home is itself a territory that in certain situations people are willing to kill or die for.

Presenting the home as a military vehicle brings to mind the centuries-old conflict between the settled way of life and the nomadic way of life. Throughout European history the nomad is commonly portrayed as a barbarian and an enemy of civilization. This image persists today, and those who practice a transient way of life in settled societies are frequently faced with opposition from the authorities and the neighboring population. In severe circumstances this can develop into a battle for survival as the alternative way of life is oppressed and threatened with extinction. The mobile home becomes a fragile out-post in a domain where it is not wanted. It does not have fortified walls or solid foundations to protect it from attack —its chief means of defense and also its greatest weapon is its mobility.

Caterpillar challenges common notions of what the home represents by knocking over a representation of a typical house and causing it to resemble a tank. The metal pipe shooting out from the pitched roof looks like both a chimney and the barrel of a gun.

"Little houses are illegal in my town," says Jay Shafer, the Iowa-based designer, builder and full-time occupant of this rolling slice of American vernacular architecture. Tumbleweed may resemble a quaint country cottage but it is every bit as tough as it is cute. The gable roof, narrow eaves and simple exterior were all designed to combat wind resistance on the road, but were actually inspired by the hardy, weather-beaten homes of Cape Cod on America's east coast. Storage space is maximized in the well-proportioned interior and transitional areas are kept to a minimum. A small porch provides an important bridge between the interior of the house and what Shafer calls the "big room," which is often a difficult boundary to egotiate in portable dwellings.

Many small mobile homes aren't suitable for year-round living and condensation is a common problem. To combat this Shafer invested in extra insulation, ensured the home was well ventilated and fitted double-glazed windows. Other than having wheels, the home is very traditional. Shafer wanted to avoid any post-occupancy problems that can occur with experimental techniques, and so stuck to traditional construction methods that have been in use for hundreds of years.

Shafer first designed Tumbleweed as a small static home to satisfy his modest needs. However, he found he would not be able to build the house in the location he wanted because it was deemed too small. "Minimum size standards," contends Shafer, "have been established to keep small dwellings from popping up and lowering the property value and prestige of larger homes in America's urban and suburban communities." In order to steer his way around the regulations Shafer mounted his home on wheels—transforming it into a travel trailer, which is governed by maximum rather than minimum size restrictions. Shafer's altercations with the law didn't end there. He wasn't able to buy a city lot on which to park his mobile home legitimately and instead had to buy another house where he could live in the garden.

Rolling Gothic is not the typical style of house you'd expect to see mounted on wheels, but Shafer had no other choice because he was prohibited from constructing a house this small in the area he wanted to live. Building the house on wheels enabled Shafer to skirt around the minimum size standards imposed on conventional dwellings.

"The scale of our homes should be as varied as the spatial needs of their inhabitants," states Shafer. "It is those needs rather than government regulations and conspicuous consumption that should determine house size."

Many of us see a wall around a wealthy estate as a barricade to keep out undesirables, but Irina Tegen's shrewd proposal turns this notion completely on its head. The architect, who won a RIBA President's Medal for the project, has transformed the boundary wall into the basic building block of her 2Guns Transportable Housing system. Tegen developed the project while studying in Johannesburg, South Africa, and designed it as a potential solution to the problem of segregation in that city's urban landscape.

The particular situation of Johannesburg and surrounding settlements such as 2Guns inspired Tegen to explore the possibilities of a modular housing system. It works along the lines of a self-assembly kit that can be transported on the back of a truck. The components are designed to be easily erected and Tegen also proposes the establishment of self-build schemes to encourage user-participation in the construction of each dwelling. The building system is flexible and can be adapted to suit the needs of the person or people hoping to use it.

Tegen suggests that the brick walls already in existence around Johannesburg's wealthy suburban enclaves are used as structural supports for the lean-to dwellings in her system. She sees the enclaves as small islands cut off from the rest of society. Their only link to the outside world is the arterial road network that leads to the city center. The 2Guns Transportable Housing system is designed to help build communities around these islands and knit them into the wider social fabric. The architect has noted how the stark division of space is already being challenged by improvized settlements and the Transportable Housing system aims to enhance this type of development.

The proposed model of development follows a similar pattern to the way many towns in Europe evolved around the fortified walls of a castle. The towns were never formally planned; they grew up at the base of a protected stronghold and gradually evolved over time. 2Guns Transportable Housing differs from the majority of projects in this book in that it is designed to encourage permanent settlements rather than fully mobile communities. Even so, the system itself is highly mobile and flexible enough to be transported from place to place.

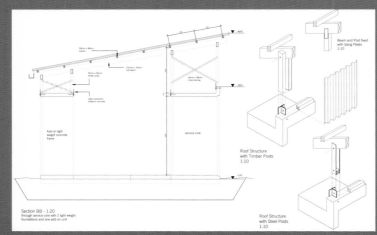

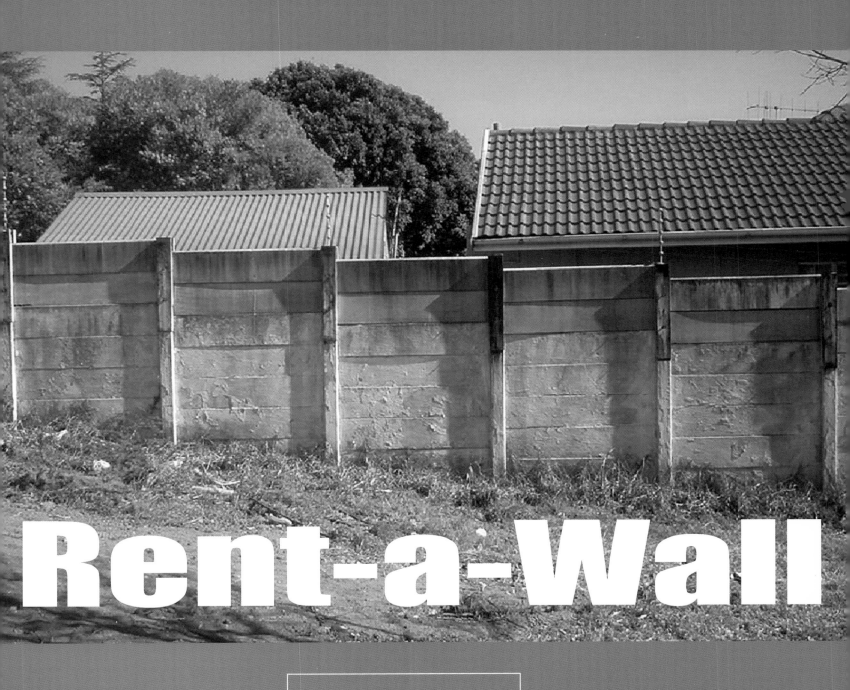

Rent-a-Wall

Defensive walls erected to keep out undesirables are revamped with a radical new function in Tegen's proposal for a transportable housing system. The architect's proposal aims to build new communities on the wasteland between the walls and the passing roads. Starter homes and commercial units assembled from ready-made kits use the walls for reinforcement, an act that transforms them from segregating barriers into instruments of inclusion.

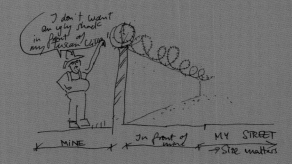

Sony Outsider is a Japanese capsule hotel room shaped to fit inside the shell of a highly mobile weapon of mass destruction. The bomb-shaped pod has many facilities in common with a capsule hotel, including a TV monitor and a DVD player, but the set up is not at all welcoming. It has more the atmosphere of a prison cell than a hotel room, and the male urinal hanging between the wash basin and the TV set adds to the impression of a correctional facility. The stark white coloring of the cell is broken by the tainted pipe running from the urinal and by images flickering across the TV screen, and is dominated by the blue Sony logo adorning the bedding. The internationally recognizable brand name also appears on the exterior of the capsule, which is a glossy white replica of the Fat Man atomic bomb dropped on Nagasaki in 1945.

Sachs highlights the similarities between the effects of war and the results of global marketing. Both can be used to impose one way of life upon another. The subtitle of Sony Outsider, *Gajin*, is Japanese for foreigner or non-Japanese national. The lifestyle encapsulated by Sony Outsider is completely manufactured. It is neither Western nor Japanese, but attempts to please both. "We don't just drop bombs," explained Sachs in an interview in March 2003, "we drop culture, and that's how we erase culture." Sachs's rendition of an atom bomb doesn't carry explosives, it carries a lifestyle dominated by in-home entertainment systems. "It's the same kind of domination and violence," he states, "just without the bullets."

Sachs is fascinated by the extraordinarily seductive power of corporate branding. In Sony Outsider the brand has taken over a dwelling and reduced it to an all-encompassing electronic gadget. The TV has become an altar and it presides over everyday activities from washing to taking a leak. Every sign of individual or regional identity has been wiped out and all that remains is a globally recognized corporate logo.

Sony Outsider (Gajin), is a life-size replica of the Fat Man atomic bomb dropped on Nagasaki during World War II. The payload in this case isn't a devastating atomic device, but a capsule hotel room fitted with a home entertainment system and a male urinal.

Mas Yendo's proposal for an Urban Living Unit is a compact container designed to offer physical and spiritual relief from the pressures of the modern metropolis. The architect describes it as an "Urban Survival Apparatus" and it is part of a series of experimental works presented by Yendo under the title Ironic Diversions.

UL-9205 is a fully portable dwelling with a footprint of only 5.5 square meters, which enables it to slot into the tightest of spaces. The unit is completely self-contained and clad in welded-steel panels to keep out external noise and air. The complex network of steel pipes on its exterior is part of a life-support system that totally isolates the unit's inhabitant from the outside world. The unique atmosphere created inside is intended to help restore the occupants' individual sense of identity from the rigors of day to day life in a nightmarish society driven by hyper-consumption.

Mas Yendo is highly critical of contemporary consumer society. Like Tom Sachs (see p. 34) Yendo fears that globalization is having an adverse affect on individual and regional identity. In the essay *Detournement* (*Experimental Diversion*) he argues that where the model

of consumer culture once promised to support individual identity it now smothers and controls it. "Diversity," he states, "has been suppressed in a systematic and pervasive manner." And he later adds: "The barrage of television-frigidaire-type technologies does little to express individual idiosyncrasy or creativity."

The architect's proposal for an autonomous and mobile living unit is an attempt to redress the balance. The dwelling is conceived as a personal space that liberates its inhabitant and places his or her own beliefs above those of the hostile society outside. Yendo refers to it as a "Zero Anxiety" space and proposes it as an antidote to the "troubling sense of rootlessness and alienation" he recognizes in the modern metropolis. UL-9205 embraces the individual and its sole function is to provide an environment tailored completely to the needs of a single occupant.

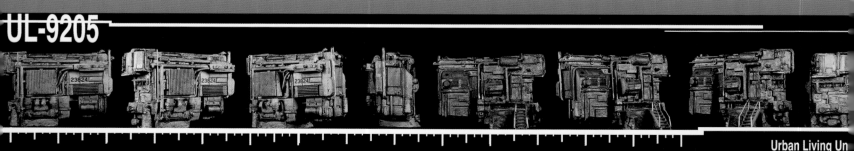

UL-9205

Urban Living Un

There is a sharp contrast in this chapter between dwellings that offer isolation and dwellings that bring people together. UL-9205 sits firmly in the first camp. The unit offers a secluded refuge from the pressures of a brutal, unrelenting city. Its workings function in time with the heartbeat of the occupant, and helps restore his or her own sense of personal identity.

Artist and activist Santiago Cirugeda creates mobile dwellings and other works that advocate challenging uses of urban space. Interventions such as Casa Insecto and Inhabited Scaffolding are specific to his hometown of Seville in southern Spain and highlight inconsistencies in the city's planning laws, inconsistencies that seem to resonate with the experiences of mobile home dwellers in cities across the western world.

Cirugeda designed and built Casa Insecto as a demountable dwelling for a tree protester. The unit was created after Seville's local authority announced plans to chop down a procession of trees that lined an attractive avenue in the city. The artist quickly identified a need for a shelter that was easy to assemble—even under cover of darkness—yet also tough enough to withstand any attempts made to dislodge it. The result is a tree-mounted structure that takes a team of four people around two hours to erect. The top half is shaped like a pitched roof and slides forwards for access and back for protection. The drum-like base is so shaped to deflect high pressure hoses, rubber missiles, and any other objects that might be launched at it.

Casa Insecto is a portable shelter for tree protesters. Its tough outer shell is shaped to foil any attempts to dislodge the unit from its strategic position among the trees.

The ongoing subversive occupation project grew from the discovery of a loophole Cirugeda discovered in Seville's planning regulations. He found that it is possible to erect scaffolding and certain other types of temporary structure for a limited period of three months without having to declare what it will be used for. The loophole was first exploited by Cirugeda to build a temporary extension to his own apartment. The materials and techniques he employed are those used all the time to build temporary support structures and workers' shelters on construction sites.

Cirugeda later applied the same method to make Puzzle House, a temporary dwelling that occupied a vacant building plot in Seville's Old Town. Such plots can remain empty for several months while the owner waits for permission to renovate a property or build a new one. The procedure is particularly drawn out in the Old Town where extensive regulations are in place to preserve the area's appearance. Cirugeda fears that these regulations are "turning [this] part of the city into an immobile and vain organism." His portable dwellings borrow the unused spaces and inject real life into an area he believes is fast becoming a theme park.

Gypsies in the UK cleverly avoided prosecution for trespass by training their dogs to catch rabbits, hares, and birds. That resourceful spirit lives on in Cirugeda's House Extension with scaffolding projects. The artist exploited a loophole in his local planning regulations that allowed him to build a temporary extension to his apartment and classify it as Scaffolding.

A demountable house designed for squatting on temporarily vacant building lots. Such spaces can remain unused for months at a time when property owners become embroiled in disputes with the town planning office. Cirugeda's transitory dwelling makes use of spaces that would otherwise be wasted.

Canadian architect A. R. Thomson first took an interest in mobile homes because they are subject to fewer regulations than their permanent counterparts. Since the mid-1990s he has worked on various types of autonomous house but found mobile dwellings offered the best scope for experimentation.

On the outside his Vanzilla mobile home is just a 1971 GMC step van, but inside it is a family home. Thomson bought the vehicle in 2001 and completely renovated it with his student loan. He fitted it with a solar panels, LED augmented lighting, and a platinum catalytic heating system. The heating system is particularly suited to small spaces as it does not emit harmful exhaust gases due to the way its propane fuel is processed, while LED lights use a fraction of the energy of a regular bulb. Thomson lived in the converted delivery van with his wife and daughter in Vancouver for about a year.

VeZaMx is Thomson's second mobile home and was renovated from a 1971 GMC / Corsair motor home. He incorporated the systems developed for Vanzilla into the new vehicle while also adding other features such as extra storage, hardwood flooring, and a propane fridge. When parked the motor home is far less conspicuous than the step van. Vancouver is home to an extensive population of RV enthusiasts who take to the roads in droves during the vacation season. Most of these vehicles are used purely for recreational purposes; however, their presence provides ample cover for those motor homes that are lived in full time. Thomson estimates that in Vancouver alone there are around 500 people residing in mobile homes. Many of these share Thomson's passion for low-energy, low-cost living outside the mainstream property market.

Thomson's miniHOME is a purpose-built low-impact dwelling that embodies his aim of making off-the-grid housing more accessible. Two versions of the home are proposed: a standard unit and an autonomous "Off-Grid Systems Package." The sloping, raised roof and timber window frames give the house the look of a conventional home and belies its status as a mobile home. Inside the tight design resembles that of a yacht and living space is maximized while energy consumption is minimized.

Vanzilla, a reconditioned GMC delivery van, was one of Thomson's first eco-RV projects. It provided a home for his family and enabled them to cut their monthly living expenses by over 50 percent. The truck is fitted with an array of energy-saving devices, and even generates its own electricity through an on board solar power system.

Many cities have bylaws that prohibit residing in a vehicle. Van dwellers have to be discreet to avoid being moved on, which can be very inconvenient at three in the morning. Thomson moved his family into VeZaMx, a GMC/Corsair motor home, because it was less conspicuous on the streets of Vancouver than the delivery van.

A. R. Thomson, Sustain, Canada
miniHOME, 2004

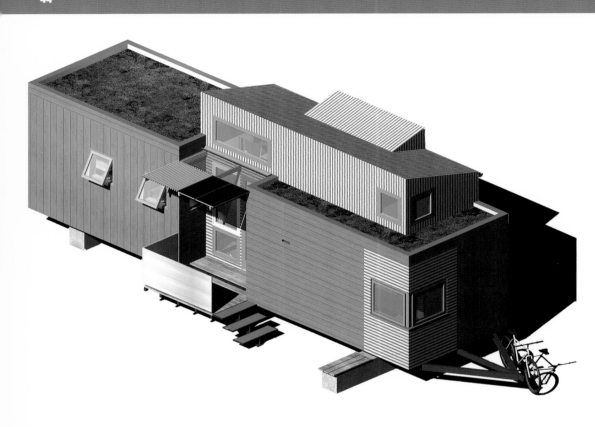

miniHOME brings together Thomson's research and experience of autonomous, low-energy dwellings. Many of the systems he developed while living in Vanzilla and VeZaMx have been integrated into this superior-quality manufactured house. Measuring 9.75 x 2.6 x 4 meters the miniHOME may be small, but its living space is extremely well organized.

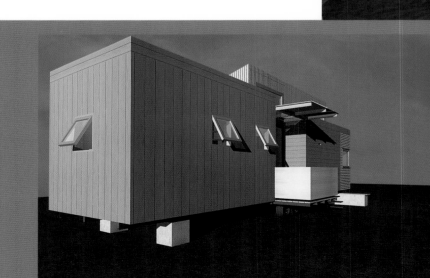

Michael Saup, Germany
Combinatoria, 2002 and ongoing

Media artist Michael Saup is wary of the rapid expansion of the digital realm. He highlights a danger that the wealth of information readily available through a computer screen may result in more and more people experiencing life through an electronic window. The internet is very liberating in its ability to keep users in touch wherever they might be, but Saup fears that it can also be used as a means to sedate and control. Online exchanges are no substitute for conversations in the physical world. Saup's Unimog enables the artist and his family to tour the real world and instigate projects wherever they go.

A further word of caution from Saup concerns our over-reliance on utility companies and fragile infrastructures that, should they collapse, might throw the world into chaos. Saup's Combinatoria gatherings, such as the one held in Karlsruhe, southern Germany in August 2003 (appropriately coinciding with a massive power cut that effectively shut down New York City), question our dependence on scarce resources and our lack of knowledge of what to do when things go wrong. The 14-day Combinatoria event provided a forum to experiment with improvised building techniques, means of obtaining food and water without relying on supermarkets, and ways of integrating new digital technologies into this atavistic way of living. A former US Army base provided the setting and resembled a post-apocalyptic scene from a *Mad Max* movie. The temporary camp sat on the demolished ruins of the Minuteman Movie Theater where American soldiers once took time out to catch the latest feature from back home.

Amongst the rubble and clumps of grass Saup and his crew erected their own silver screen by covering a wall of beer crates with white tarpaulin. Visitors used it to give presentations and show short films to an audience seated on bleachers made from wooden pallets to create an improvised amphitheater. Tents, Saup's Unimog, and other vehicles provided the sleeping quarters while the kitchen and a long table, which doubled up as a dining area and work station, were sheltered by metal fencing and a large fabric canopy. The event brought people together to share information, learn new skills, and experience a different way of living.

Michael Saup is the Professor for Digital Media Arts at the Department of New Media at the ZKM Hochschule für Gestaltung in Karlsruhe. His Unimog truck plays a vital role in his research, which takes the artist into communities all over the world. The Combinatoria events are nomadic workshops that bring people together to share ideas and learn from direct experience and participation rather than through a computer screen.

Michael Saup, Germany
Combinatoria, 2002 and ongoing

Bleachers built with wooden pallets and beer crates provided a place to sit while watching presentations and a place to sleep when the weather allowed.

Flexible Friends

1234

Lucy Orta, UK/France
M. I. U. VI, 2002

A large part of Lucy Orta's work is about making connections; both physical and social. Since the early 1990s the artist has pioneered highly influential works that bring together the disciplines of art, performance, architecture, and fashion. The theme of connection is maintained right down to the details of her survival outfits and shelters, which are fitted with zip fasteners, plastic clips, Velcro and other linking devices that form physical bonds.

M. I. U. VI is the sixth work in a series of Mobile Intervention Units and when exhibited together the individual pieces form the Mobile Intervention Convoy. M. I. U. VI consists of a trailer with six of Orta's survival sacks laid in pairs on stretchers that form three separate decks. A ladder provides access to each of the decks and the unit is topped with a triangular metal frame resembling the pitched roof of a house or church, which emphasizes its function as a refuge.

The shiny surface of the metal trailer and the aluminum fabric used on the survival sacks creates mirrors that reflect the M. I. U. VI's surroundings and make yet more connections with its immediate environment. The reflective fabric used on the exterior of the survival sacks is there to deflect sunlight and prevent the occupant from overheating. When applied to the inside the material holds in body heat and helps maintain a stable temperature. Other fabrics used include Kevlar and microporous rip-stop nylon, a material that breathes and also helps keep the body in a comfortable condition.

While part of the Mobile Intervention Convoy the M. I. U. VI trailer can be connected to one of Orta's reconfigured military ambulances. The vehicles, although once employed by the military, are not war machines. They are rescue vehicles designed to bring aid to victims too injured or too sick to help themselves. The arrangement of empty survival sacks on the M. I. U. VI trailer and the pointed metal frame bears some resemblance to a war memorial. It looks haunting while it stands unoccupied in a gallery or museum. However, the unit has the function of a life-saving apparatus that promotes survival and wellbeing.

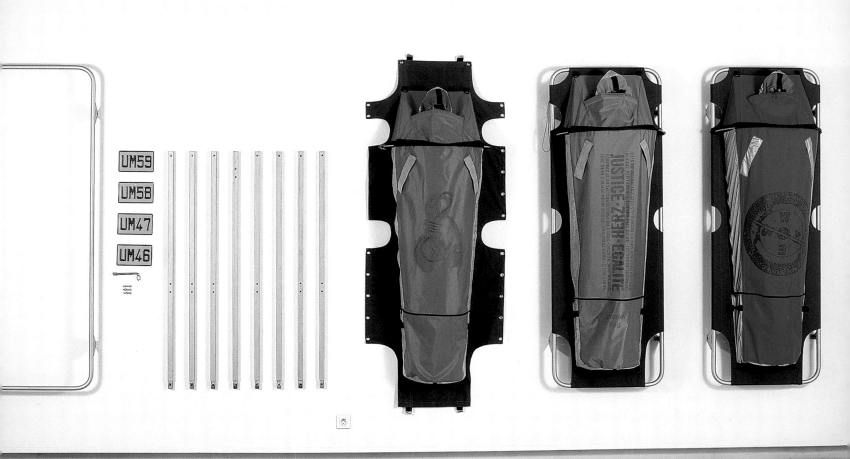

M.I.U. VI, Kit, 2002. Trailer, camp beds, ladder, Kevlar, diverse fabrics, silkscreen print, telescopic aluminum structure, number plates. Here, the individual components that make up the Mobile Intervention Unit have been dismantled or disconnected and hung on the museum wall.

Lucy Orta, UK/France
M.I.U. VI, 2002

54

M.I.U. VI, 2002. The complex fabrics used to make the individual Survival Sacks are combined to offer the greatest level of comfort to the person inside. The material used has a microporous-membrane coating that allows moisture to pass from the inside out but not the other way around. A special coating across the surfaces that come into contact with the body minimizes abrasions during transit, while reflective and luminescent fabrics on the outside offer protection and act as highly visible warning signs.

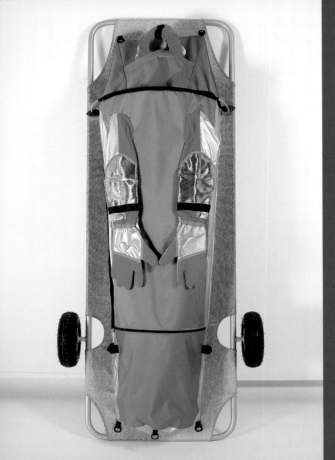

The So-an / Mobile Chanoyu Room is a prime example of Toshihiko Suzuki's ability to update traditional Japanese architecture using modern technology. The room derives from the special spaces associated with Chanoyu or Way of the Tea, the Japanese art of preparing and serving tea. *So-an* is the name given to the simple, rustic style that has been associated with the Way of the Tea since the 16th century. Suzuki carefully marries this traditional aesthetic with materials such as aluminum honeycomb panels coated in rice paper. Incorporated into the wall panels are small lights that cause the paper covering to glow and follow a gentle sequence of illumination. The whole room can be dismantled and packed away into a set of fifteen carry cases for transportation or storage.

Mobile Ichijyo 1 and 2 are also portable rooms dedicated to the preparation of tea, only smaller than So-an / Mobile Chanoyu Room. An *ichijyo* is the area covered by a single tatami mat, which traditionally is enough room to sleep. The first Mobile Ichijyo is exceptionally beautiful and resembles a simple paper lantern.

It folds out of an aluminum carry-case, which splits to form the floor and ceiling of the room. A curtain of white mosquito net hanging between the ceiling and base separates the space inside from the public realm. The second incarnation of the Mobile Ichijyo also opens from a flat case and covers the same floor area as the first. However, instead of using a screen to create an intimate space Mobile Ichijyo 2 has a shelter made from a complex array of cables, tubes, and fabric.

The tea rooms work in conjunction with a large portable shelter Suzuki devised for his Atelier in a Mountain. The shelter sits beside Suzuki's 1963 Globe Trotter Airstream trailer on a patch of land he leased in the mountains of Yamagata, Japan. Because of a clause in his lease, Suzuki is not permitted to build anything that will leave a mark on the site when eventually he vacates it. His solution is the Atelier in a Mountain, a fully portable live / work space that can be dismantled and moved to a new location without leaving a trace of its existence.

Mobile ICHIJYO/1 is a portable tea room that packs away into an aluminum case. The roof is suspended from above by a series of cables hooked on to nearby supports. A translucent curtain creates an intimate room for quiet contemplation with enough space for one person to conduct a traditional tea ceremony.

Mobile ICHIJYO/2 covers the same floor space as its predecessor (one tatami mat or ichijyo), but it creates a separated environment through a system of cloth canopies, cables, and tubes.

Toshihiko Suzuki, Japan
SO-AN / Mobile Chanoyu Room, 2000
Atelier in a Mountain, 1998 and ongoing

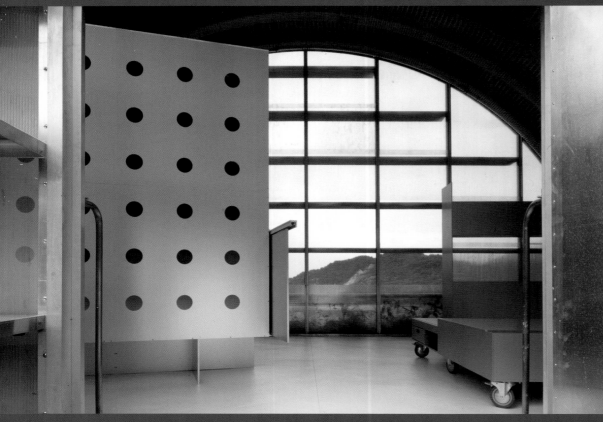

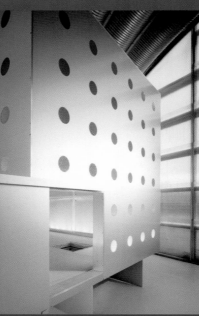

Suzuki's Atelier in a Mountain consists of an aluminum shelter and an Airstream trailer, which the architect fitted out with a new floor and furniture. The shelter is constructed from precisely cut aluminum panels that are light enough to be lifted by only two people.

Sa-an/Mobile Chanoyu Room is a collapsible tea room made from aluminum honeycomb panels. The assembled structure measures 2 square meters and is mounted 30 cm above ground to allow room for the fireplace installation. Lights mounted inside the honeycomb panels cause the room to glow and are programmed to follow a delicate pattern that appears to continually flow around the walls.

Moreno Ferrari has created a series of garments that transform into instant, take-anywhere shelters. Tent (p. 62) is a long white hooded coat that transforms into an urban igloo. It is made from rubberized rip-stop nylon, a material that gives protection from both wind and rain. Parka/Air Mattress is a bright blue polyurethane coat that converts into an inflatable bed. It comes with an air compressor, torch, and a fine nylon mesh tent supported by telescopic carbon rods. The two instant dwellings respond to a desire for a familiar space that can counteract anxious feelings brought on by new and unfamiliar locations.

Tent and Parka / Air Mattress are clothes or shelters for individuals but Serra (Greenhouse) (p. 63) is an inflatable structure formed by the coming together of three hooded coats: one for a mother, one for a father, and one for a child. It is a jigsaw of separate parts that together form a soft shelter supported by a framework of air-filled tubes. As a greenhouse is a fertile environment where plants are nurtured, nourished, and protected from the elements, similarly Ferrari's Serra is a space of well-being and relaxation. Where Tent and Parka/Air Mattress are very urban and dynamic in appearance, Serra is decorated with a soft, natural pattern inspired by delicate butterfly wings.

Ferrari's outfits are made with semi-transparent material that switches attention away from the object itself to the person inside. It can also act as a kind of camouflage that causes the outfit to merge into its surroundings. The designer states that the transformable clothes were inspired by ideals such as self-sufficiency, individual freedom, and defending one's dreams. The spaces formed by his clothes are highly personal enclosures that encourage imaginative thinking and quiet contemplation.

Parka/Air-Mattress is made from waterproof polyurethane that can be inflated to transform it into an air bed. The garment comes with a pump, a small torch, and a fine nylon tent supported by telescopic carbon rods.

Moreno Ferrari, Italy

Tent (for C. P. Company), 2001
Serra (Greenhouse / Jigsaw), 2002

Tent is a long hooded cloak manufactured from rubberized, wind- and rainproof rip-stop nylon. Carbon rods provide the support structure for the tent, which is formed by using zip fasteners to convert the cloak into a canopy.

Air-filled tubes form the structure of Serra (Greenhouse/Jigsaw), which, when not inflated, is a three-meter-long roll of fabric. The material has three anoraks zipped into it and is decorated with a pattern inspired by butterfly wings.

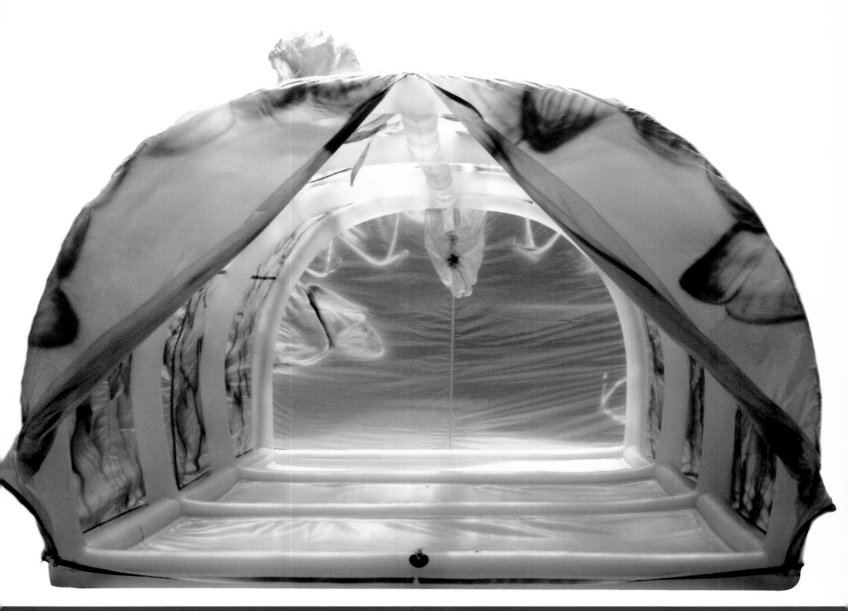

Oskar Leo Kaufmann, Austria
Carton House, 2002

Architect Oskar Leo Kaufmann has built a strong reputation for his innovative approach to prefabricated buildings. Carton House is a departure from the sophisticated finish of Kaufmann's other portable houses such as Su-Si (2000) and Oa-Sys (2003), but its charming appearance captures perfectly the architect's passion for mobile dwellings.

Carton House is a small cardboard house that folds out from a hand-held carry case. Each case comes wrapped in a colored plastic sheet that can also be used as a protective cover for the completed house. Instructions demonstrating how to assemble the foldaway dwelling are printed on the plastic wrapper and, if followed, the house should be up and ready to use in three minutes. It weighs just 12 kilogrammes and when unfolded measures 2 × 1 × 1.75 meters. There is enough room inside for one adult to lie down quite comfortably and the cardboard floor gives some insulation against cold from the ground below.

Fifty Carton Houses were deployed on the streets of Turin, Italy during the city's Biennale Arte Emergente in 2002. It is shaped to resemble a typical house and acts as a symbol of home. The witty design is accessible and instantly appealing. Assembling the house is like a puzzle or a game and the finished object looks very much like a child's playhouse. However, Carton House also alludes to the cardboard dwellings put together by homeless people and Kaufmann has suggested that it could be used as a basic shelter for sleeping on the streets. The idea that the Carton House can be both a plaything and an essential shelter may not sit comfortably for some, but it illustrates the enormous range of perceptions we have of the place we call home.

The small folding house is pictured at Big Torino 2002, the Biennale Arte Emergente, Turin, Italy. Carton House folds away into a case measuring 85 x 56 x 16 cm and can be reassembled in a matter of minutes.

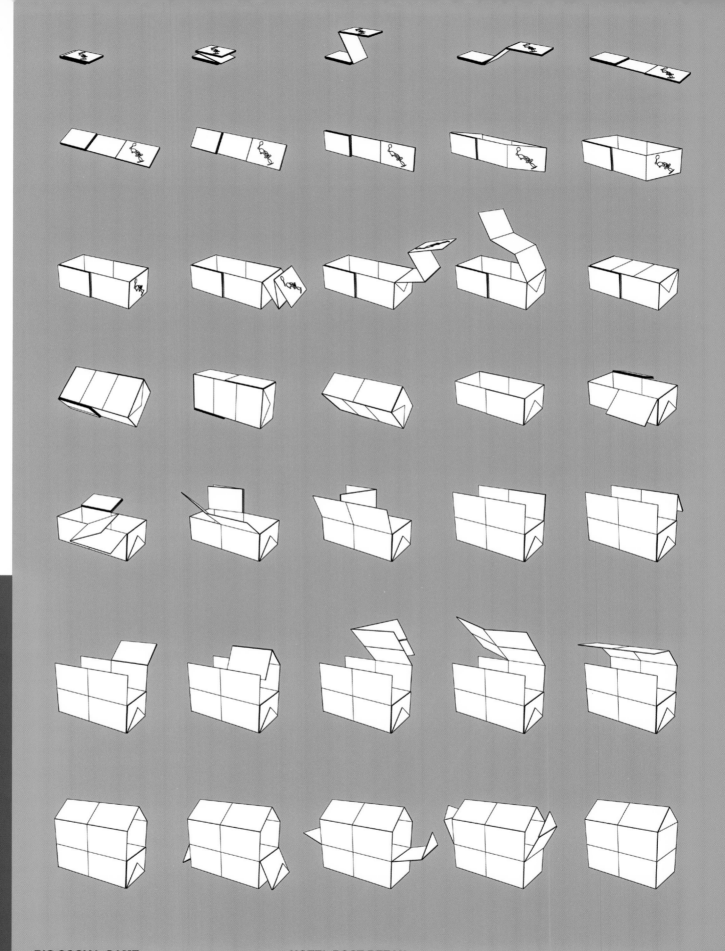

It's a **BIG SOCIAL GAME** BIG TORINO 2002 www.bigtorino.net / sponsored by **HOTEL POST BEZAU** www.hotelpostbezau.com / designed by OSKAR LEO KAUFMANN www.olk.cc / produced by FLATZ www.flatz.com

Kosuke Tsumura, Japan
Final Home, 1991 and ongoing
Home Room (in collaboration with Idée), 2000

66

Final Home was the name given to an extraordinary garment first presented by fashion designer Kosuke Tsumura in 1992. Tsumura developed the concept further and gradually built a brand around the idea of clothing that adapts and transforms to different needs. The designer asked himself what type of clothes he would produce to aid survival if he were to lose his own home, and came up with Final Home as a response. He experimented with further designs and spent a night on the streets in 1993 wearing the third version of the outfit to test and improve its functionality. Final Home for Tsumura means the ultimate shelter and the garments represent a fusion of clothing and accommodation.

The clothes are covered with zip-fastened pockets that can be stuffed with anything from ripped-up newspaper for added insulation to emergency food and medical supplies. When not needed as a tool for survival the pockets can be used like any other to store train tickets, a camera, or a cellular phone. There is a distinct urban feel to the Final Home outfits but clothing more associated with remote rural areas such as a marksman's jacket or a soldier's utility pants play a major influence, as do the improvised methods employed to keep warm and dry by homeless individuals.

Home Room is an extension to the Final Home clothing line and is more obviously recognizable as a form of shelter. It is designed along similar lines to the clothing in that the fabric used to cover the tubular frame also contains zip fastened pockets. Extra protection from falling objects, perhaps for use in an earthquake situation, is given by roll bars that cross the rear and top of the shelter.

Clothing for the apocalypse is an appropriate description of Final Home. The outfits are designed as mobile homes that aid survival in post-disaster situations, such as a city reduced to rubble by an earthquake or bomb blast. Each garment is covered with pockets that can be stuffed and expanded with newspaper for added insulation and cushioning; or with food, water, and medical supplies to transform it into a survival kit.

Home Room applies the philosophy behind Final Home's clothing to a portable shelter. Tsumura, along with other designers such as Moreno Ferrari, and the artist Lucy Orta, creates clothing that offers protection from disasters. On first impression there's an alarming sense of dread for the future in his work, but this is sharply counteracted by a firm belief that adversity can be defeated by ingenuity.

Do-Ho Suh, Korea
Seoul Home / L. A. Home / N. Y. Home / Baltimore Home / London Home / Seattle Home, 1999

Seoul Home... is the first in a series of works by Korean artist Do-Ho Suh that explore the meaning of home. While studying in New York Do-Ho Suh lived in an apartment just across the street from a fire station. The noise of the sirens often kept him awake at night and caused the artist to think of the last time he had a decent night's sleep. He thought about his former bedroom in his family's home in Korea and started thinking of ways to recreate that space in his New York apartment. Do-Ho Suh hit upon the idea of making the house entirely out of fabric and eventually realized the project for an exhibition at the Korean Cultural Center in Los Angeles. *Seoul Home...* is an incredibly detailed replica of Suh's family home. Many different stitches used in traditional Korean dress-making were employed to join the cuts of fabric and recreate the details of the house. "For me, dressmaking is like architecture," stated the artist in an interview with Lisa G. Corrin in 2002. "When you expand this idea of clothing as a space, it becomes an inhabitable structure, a building, a house made of fabric."

Do-Ho Suh was invited to take part in the *My Home is Yours. Your Home is Mine* exhibition at the Rodin Gallery in Seoul, South Korea. He was living in New York at the time and decided to recreate his apartment there and transport it to Korea. *Apartment 348...* (pp. 70–71) is a precise replica of the artist's New York apartment made in the same manner as *Seoul Home*. Details including light switches, door handles, and water faucets are all painstakingly recreated to give a vivid impression of the actual building.

Do-Ho Suh compares *Seoul Home...* to a parachute that has helped cushion his landing in a new and different culture. The house can be packed into a suitcase and enables the artist to carry his childhood memories with him wherever he goes. The piece deals with issues of loss and separation whereas *Apartment 348...* expresses Suh's desire to move on and overcome the differences between the culture of his past and the culture of his present.

Seoul Home / L. A. Home / New York Home / Baltimore Home / London Home / Seattle Home / L. A. Home, 1999. Silk and metal armatures, 149 x 240 x 240 inches.

The Gilbert B. Friesen Visitors' Gallery

Do-Ho Suh, Korea

348 West 22nd Street, Apartment A, New York, N.Y. 10011 at Rodin Gallery Seoul / Tokyo Opera City Art Gallery / Serpentine Gallery, London / Biennale of Sydney / Seattle Art Museum, 2001

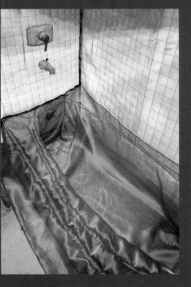

Every time Seoul Home... is exhibited in a new city the artist adds the name of that city to the title of the piece. He repeated this ongoing readjustment of the title with Apartment 348... and this reflects the way the pieces are adapted to each new space.

The immediate difference between Seoul Home... and Apartment 348... is the division of interior space. Compared to the openness of Seoul Home..., Apartment 348... is a jungle of walls and corridors.

Gregorio Brugnoli-Errázuriz and students at the Architecture School, Faculty of Architecture and Urbanism, Universidad Central de Chile, Santiago, Chile

Emergency Modules A, C, and E, 2002

The Emergency Modules are a series of instant dwellings designed for situations where traditional construction techniques are just too slow, such as shanty settlements and squats. This precarious occupation of land carries with it the ever present danger of forced eviction, which can leave people without even the most basic type of shelter. The materials used to manufacture the Emergency Modules are practical, inexpensive, and readily available. All five dwellings are built using plastic tubes for the structural framework and various types of plastic sheeting as a skin.

Module A is essentially an open cubic space with smaller, private compartments projecting from its sides. A transparent skin covers the core area. but opaque black plastic is used to provide privacy around the sleeping bunk and dressing room. Square frames made from the plastic tubing make up Module A's framework. The plastic sheeting hangs from this frame and expands and contracts like bellows. The sleeping bunk is raised above the ground and can also be folded away in this manner when not needed.

Modules B and D are a mixture of public and private spaces defined by opaque screens. The screens shield parts of the modules from public view and can be rearranged as needed. A dining table and bench are built into Module B using the pipes and thick vinyl sheets. Module C is the only one to be coated with patterned fabric. One of its walls opens out to form an awning. Neat square frames form the strong-looking structure of Module E, and the whole unit collapses down to be as wide as its bed.

Emergency Module A by Carolina Castillo, Juan José Leguina, Felipe Godoy, Diego Yurjevic, Eduardo Garate, and Carmen Aguilar.

Emergency Module E by Suzette Steger, Nicolás Madariaga, Constanza Santibáñez, Andrea Pérez, Héctor Matamala, and Rodrigo Haverbeck.

Emergency Module C by Carla Barría, Daniel Toloza, David Barrios, Maria José Valenzuela, Catalina Millán Silva, and Francisco Ramírez.

Gregorio Brugnoli-Errázuriz and students at the Architecture School,
Faculty of Architecture and Urbanism, Universidad Central de Chile, **Santiago, Chile**
Emergency Modules B, and D, 2002

74

Emergency Module D by Eduardo Basaure, Rodrigo Rojas, Richard
Rivano, Cristian Chadid, and Bárbara Morgado.

Emergency Module B by Paloma González, Harry Fieldhouse,
Loreto Arce, Pablo Alvarez, Rodrigo Buron, Aarón Fernández,
and Octavio Ulloa.

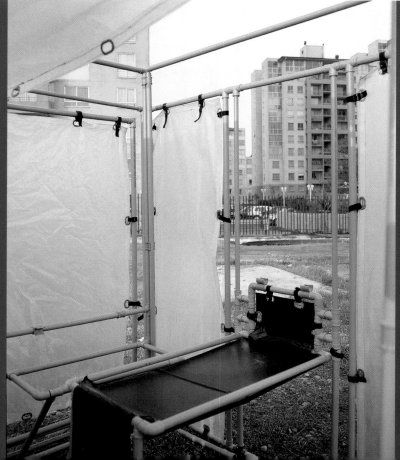

Anybody who has spent nights sleeping on the floor of a friend's apartment will appreciate Matali Crasset's When Jim Comes to Paris. The hospitality tower was inspired by the cramped studio apartments of Paris and is designed to make overnight guests feel welcome—even when the host has a minimum amount of space to offer.

The floor-standing column of gray tufted felt unzips to create a base for a mattress that is rolled up inside. For some designers this would be an ample solution to the fold-out bed, but not for Crasset. She has considered other needs of her guests and included a personal lamp and an alarm clock, just in case Jim forgets his own.

Téo From 2 to 3 is a similar device in that it provides a temporary place for rest. However, the "siesta stool" is designed for taking naps in the work place rather than the home. The mattress and pillow wrap around a small holding pole when not in use and take up about as much space as a waste-paper bin. When unrolled, a large donut-shaped sign reading "DO NOT DISTURB" is fixed to the top of the pole to alert colleagues that someone is having a snooze.

Neither When Jim Comes to Paris nor Téo From 2 to 3 incorporate a physical shelter into their design, but when in use they employ other means to distinguish the space around them. Crasset's Popup Space is a physical shelter in which a dome-like shape can be hoisted up from a flat mat on the floor. Like When Jim Comes to Paris and Téo From 2 to 3, Popup Space seems ideally suited to a room of limited size, which it is able to transform into a space entirely different. The impersonal nature of small apartments and offices can make it difficult to find space for yourself, let alone a guest. Crasset's designs overcome that dilemma and provide guests with a space of their own.

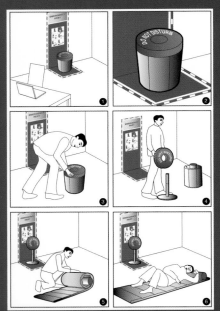

Téo from 2 to 3, 1999
Siesta Stool
Open: 10 x 180 x 45 cm
Closed diameter: 52 x 40 cm
Structure in wood, inside in foam bi-density high-resilience
Outside cover: Coated fabric, double-tufted felt

Popup Space, 2002
Interior Yurt
Closed: 3 x 400 x 400 cm; Opened: 230 x 400 x 400 cm
On the principle of Oritapi, a living space that expands
or withdraws
View of Matali Crasset's exhibition, Un Pas de Coté
91/02, at MU.DAC – Lausanne, Switzerland.

When Jim Comes to Paris, 1995
Hospitality Tower
when open: 10 x 190 x 130 cm; when closed:
190 x 34 x 34 cm (without lamp and alarm clock)
Structure: Tufted felt and foam bi-density high-
resilience. Mattress cover and inside: cotton.

MIKRO-House and MIKRO-City are miniature worlds etched, cut and folded from paper-thin sheets of stainless steel. Buxton manufactured the 3D depictions of home with a process known as chemical milling in which acid is used to eat away at designated patterns marked on each metal sheet. The technique is incredibly precise and has been used for many years to engineer tiny components for the electronics industry. It is also inexpensive and quick to produce, which makes it ideal for experimentation.

MIKRO-House arrives as four flat sheets of precut stainless steel. Out of these sheets fold all the components that make up each of the four "rooms" comprising a lounge, a bathroom, a kitchen, and a bedroom. Buxton has built an original depiction of the home by grouping together the objects we interact with everyday from remote control handsets and video games to shower gel and toilet paper.

The milling technique employed is intricate and precise but Buxton balances out the machine-made perfection by adding tell-tale signs of everyday life. A dirty knife and fork, for instance, lie unwashed in the kitchen sink and a small puddle of water hasn't quite drained from the bath tub. Such details pull the viewer further into the tiny house and build a story about its absent occupant—a story that is given a bizarre twist by a pair of handcuffs left hanging from the bed. Buxton expanded on the ideas in MIKRO-House to build MIKRO-City for the Design Museum in London. Towers, also cut from stainless steel, create the pattern of an urban grid into which slot the individual apartments, office spaces and a hospital.

The HUB Craft Centre Project enabled Buxton to apply the same techniques used in his miniatures to a full-size scenario. The chamber, which is used to house a public access database in a craft center in rural Lincolnshire, was transported as eight flat sheets of laser-cut stainless steel. The walls of the room and all the furniture inside were assembled from these eight sheets of metal and two additional acrylic panels that form the seats of the chairs and the desk-top areas. The coat hangers and hanging rack first seen in MIKRO-House make an appearance here as does a magazine rack and a bottle opener—all cut and folded from the flat metal panels.

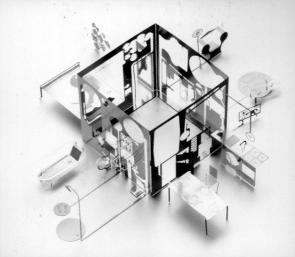

Far left: Hub Craft Centre Project, Sleaford, Lincolnshire, UK, 2003. Laser-cut 2.5 mm stainless steel with the furniture inside cut from the walls of the cube. 230 cm square.

Mikro-City, 2003. Living in a Tank installation, Design Museum, London, July – September 2003. Laser cut and chemical milled stainless steel. Eating, sleeping, working, playing, bathing, and gardening represent the themes incorporated into Mikro-City. The structure is a miniature cityscape or urban grid. Tiny details including CCTV cameras, cyclists, satellite dishes, and HVAC ducts bolster that impression and engage the viewer. The towers provide a network of boxes that house apartments, a hospital, and an office.

Left: Mikro-House, 2002. Chemical milled, 150 micron stainless steel, central cube part is 8 cm square. References to the work of influential designers such as Ron Arad sit alongside everyday objects such as a set of bathroom scales and a rubber tree plant in Buxton's Mikro-House. The designer has also managed to include miniature examples of his other work such as the dining table and chair in the fold-out kitchen.

Hans-Walter Müller has been at the forefront of inflatable art and architecture since the early 1960s. The German-born architect first experimented with air-filled forms while working with light shows and projected images in the Paris Museum of Modern Art. What started out as a new type of screen for Müller's projections rapidly evolved into a source of constant fascination. Huge air-supported theaters, circus tents, exhibition halls, an aviary, and even a church are just a selection of the magnificent mobile buildings Müller has created, but his endless passion for inflatables is perhaps best expressed by his own home.

Müller's multicolored home sits at the edge of a forest in La Ferté-Alais, just south of Paris, and although the house has remained at this location since 1971, it is the foremost example of a living and breathing home to be built using inflatable technology. The unique house covers a floor area of 210 square meters and the ceiling reaches over four meters high. The space also functions as Müller's workshop and Laurence Falzon, writing in the book *Air-Air*, describes it as a "haven of experiment, moored to the rocks and transparent to the vegetation around." The surrounding trees cast shadows across its walls and create an ever-changing pattern of light and shade inside. "The walls become living walls," wrote Müller in *Technique et Architecture* in 1975, "changing with the time of day." In the same piece Müller described inflatable architecture as a "new construction that has nothing in common with any construction of the past" and declared the architecture of the post and lintel "finished."

Inflatable buildings were first developed in the 1940s by an engineer named Walter W. Bird for the US Air Force, which needed a fine yet sturdy mobile shelter to house its sensitive radar apparatus. Bird, together with other pioneers of inflatable structures, R. Buckminster Fuller and Frei Otto, proved a major influence on radical architecture collectives that emerged in the 1960s. Groups including Archigram in the UK, Utopie in France, and Coop Himmelb(l)au and Haus-Rucker-Co from Austria all experimented with prototype inflatable dwellings, but none went anywhere near as far as Hans-Walter Müller. His inflatable home is a magical reminder of the considerable potential of this often neglected construction technology.

Hans-Walter Müller, Germany/France
Inflatable House/Studio, 1971

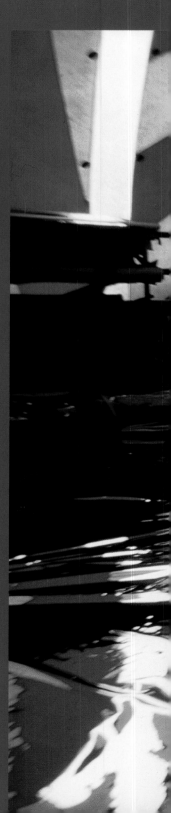

Hans-Walter Müller's inflatable home/studio, La Ferté-Alais, first erected in 1971. Despite its bright colors the house is barely noticeable among the surrounding trees. Inside, the trees form moving patterns across the walls. In 1975 Müller built other, much smaller inflatable houses for tramps sleeping rough in the tunnels of the Paris Metro system. The shelters sat on ventilation shafts and were filled with the warm air from below.

Taking the Trai

ler Park Uptown

1234

Patkau Architects Inc., Canada
La Petite Maison de Weekend, 2001

The traditional holiday home is given a thorough reworking by Patkau Architects' elegant portable dwelling, La Petite Maison de Weekend. This attractive house is designed to have as little impact on the environment as possible and is built mostly with natural materials. Crafted like a large piece of furniture, La Petite Maison incorporates a sleeping loft, deep storage cupboard, kitchenette, and shower room under a sloping roof. The intricate arrangement of the different areas maximizes the limited space available and the whole piece is unified by the extensive use of wood.

The architects designed the attractive wooden house to be almost self-sufficient and it serves as a fully working prototype for other such dwellings. A fabric reservoir running along the lower edge of the roof collects and distributes rainwater while a composting toilet is used to process waste. Photovoltaic cells installed on the roof convert solar energy into electricity, which is stored within four batteries. The batteries power the unit's lighting, a high efficiency refrigerator, and a small fan in the toilet.

The house is constructed primarily from renewable or recyclable materials. Hemlock spruce is used for the structure and paneling of the house with steel reinforcements applied where needed. The wood was chosen for its natural beauty and ability to perform structurally. The large roof measures approximately 4.3 × 6 meters and is fabricated from glass and steel. It reaches out beyond the confines of the house and forms a shelter around the dwelling's perimeter, which opens up the interior space and makes it seem even more inviting. There are no physical barriers to separate or define the boundary between the external and interior space of La Petite Maison. It is an outside room that merges with its surroundings.

The ladder provides access to the enclosed sleeping areas in the upper half of the house. The sack-like reservoir used to collect rainwater can be seen hanging below the sloping roof.

Made almost entirely of hemlock spruce, La Petite Maison de Weekend is an intricately arranged living space that makes the most of its limited dimensions.

Werner Aisslinger's Loftcube is a portable penthouse that enables high-flying executives to live among the pigeons. The stylish living pod is reminiscent of Matti Suuronen's Futuro House and other space-age bachelor pads of the 1960s. It was designed to rest on city-center roof tops and its modular construction means that it can be transported and assembled with relative ease. For the super-rich, however, the architect suggests a helicopter as the ideal method for moving the unit from place to place.

The Loftcube is necessarily compact with a floor area of only 36 square meters but contains all the comforts of a deluxe hotel room. The outer walls are made up of individual panels available in opaque, translucent, or transparent and can be varied according to the needs of the user. The pristine yet functional interior features a kitchen, bathroom, and living and sleeping areas and the

limitations imposed by size have resulted in a number of space-saving innovations. A dual-purpose faucet integrated into the slender dividing wall between the bathroom and living area can be levered to water plants or to be used as a shower head. Similarly, the faucet in the panel between the kitchen and bathroom serves both the kitchen sink and the bathroom wash basin.

The soft-cornered outer shell of the dwelling sits upon four supporting legs and almost looks like it is hovering, an appearance well suited to its rooftop location. Aisslinger envisages the emergence of whole new roof-top communities as more property developers realize the potential of these under-used spaces. The Loftcube enables people to live right in the heart of vibrant cities, yet its serene appearance also creates a space that can act as a lofty retreat above the commotion and noise of busy city streets.

Loftcube aims to make living on roof tops just as fashionable as living in a loft.
Aisslinger sculpted the lavish dwelling from DuPont's latest materials. It is pictured
here beside the River Spree in Berlin.

The shower head is fitted with a lever so it can also be used to water the plants.
Similarly, the faucet over the kitchen sink also serves the wash basin in the bathroom.

Atelier van Lieshout, Netherlands
Maxi Capsule Luxus, 2002

"It's like we're farming people," says Joep van Lieshout of the Mini Capsule Side Entrance, "I like it because it reminds me of the rabbit hutch we had on the farm." The farm was part of a free state Atelier van Lieshout (AVL) established in the port of Rotterdam in 2001. Lieshout founded AVL in 1995 and it has since developed into a flourishing company operating in the areas of art, design, and architecture. All buildings produced by the firm are portable and the Free State it created in Rotterdam, known as AVL-Ville, even included a mobile farm, but this and all the other facilities including a power plant, hospital and restaurant were removed when the project was shut down in November 2001.

AVL's numerous Mini Capsules are basic solutions for the storage of people. Mini Capsule Side Entrance (p.92) is reminiscent of the Japanese capsule hotels that came to prominence in the late 1970s. Each tiny room is fitted with a bed, a lamp, a window, clothing hooks and an electrical outlet. Maxi Capsule Luxus is far more opulent and boasts added insulation, heating, air conditioning, a TV and sound system, mini-bar, and seating pit. However, despite all its extra trimmings, Maxi Capsule Luxus essentially performs the same function as the other Mini Capsules in that it provides shelter around a bed.

The bed plays a central role in all the capsules. Even in Maxi Capsule Luxus there are no other practical fittings such as a wash basin, toilet, or shower. Beds provide the focus in many of AVL's mobile homes and are often accompanied by a plentiful supply of booze, which is usually present to fuel sexual activity. They are presented as places to sleep, dream, relax and indulge in all manner of sexual acts. Maxi Capsule Luxus appears especially suited to amorous liaisons. Its mini-fridge is perfect for storing beer and wine while all the interior and exterior surfaces are finished in bright red, the color most associated with passion and action.

Maxi Capsule Luxus, 2002. Fiberglass, mixed media.

AVL often designs its dwellings from the inside out, which results in unusual protrusions like those on the exterior of Maxi Capsule Luxus. The small domes contain the stereo speakers while the flexible tubes leading into the two boxes carry electricity cables to the mini-fridge and TV set.

Atelier van Lieshout

Mini Capsule Beige, 2001
Mini Capsule Blue, 2002
Mini Capsule Side Entrance, 2002

Inspired by rabbit hutches and Japanese capsule hotels, AVL's Mini Capsules look like small huts designed for the intensive farming of people.

Mini Capsule Side Entrance (6 units), 2002. Fiberglass, mixed media.

Mini Capsule Blue, 2002.
Fiberglass, mixed media.

Mini Capsule Beige, 2001.
Fiberglass, mixed media.

Office of Mobile Design's (OMD) Portable House concept is a revision of a proposal first presented in 2001. The mobile home is similar to the Loftcube (see p. 88) and M-House (see p. 98) in that it mixes up the versatility of the trailer home with the styling of a fashionable apartment. Jennifer Siegal, the founder of OMD, challenges preconceived notions of the trailer park and has created Portable House as a "provocative counterpoint" to the assumptions of the mainstream housing market.

A primary aim for the Portable House is to make the fullest use of sustainable building materials. The interior partitions are made with fiberboard derived from recycled waste paper, the flooring is made from bamboo, Polygal (a transparent, ribbed plastic) is used in place of glass, and structural wall paneling is used for its added insulation properties. Central to the Portable House is its kitchen and bathroom facility, which also serves as a division between the sleeping area and the lounge.

The compact house can be enlarged when extra space is needed by sliding out and extending the structure containing the lounge area. Multiple Portable Houses can be combined to create yet more living space or be reconfigured to serve other functions.

OMD is based in Los Angeles, a city where many buildings are just temporary fixtures constructed to serve a limited purpose and then demolished. Thus the city is littered with unsightly, rubble-covered lots waiting to be filled by yet another disposable structure. The whole process seems completely absurd when there are so many portable solutions that could be employed instead. The Eco-Ville project aims to transform an area of downtown Los Angeles with the deployment of approximately 40 of OMD's Portable House modules. The houses will be converted into live/work spaces to form a creative, mixed-use village that highlights the potential of modern developments based on the model of the trailer park.

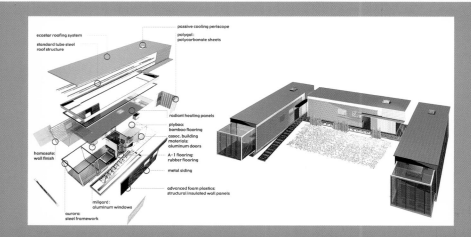

Individual Portable House modules can be connected with others to create an expanded living space or a home/office. The house rests lightly in the landscape and is adaptable to a variety of environments.

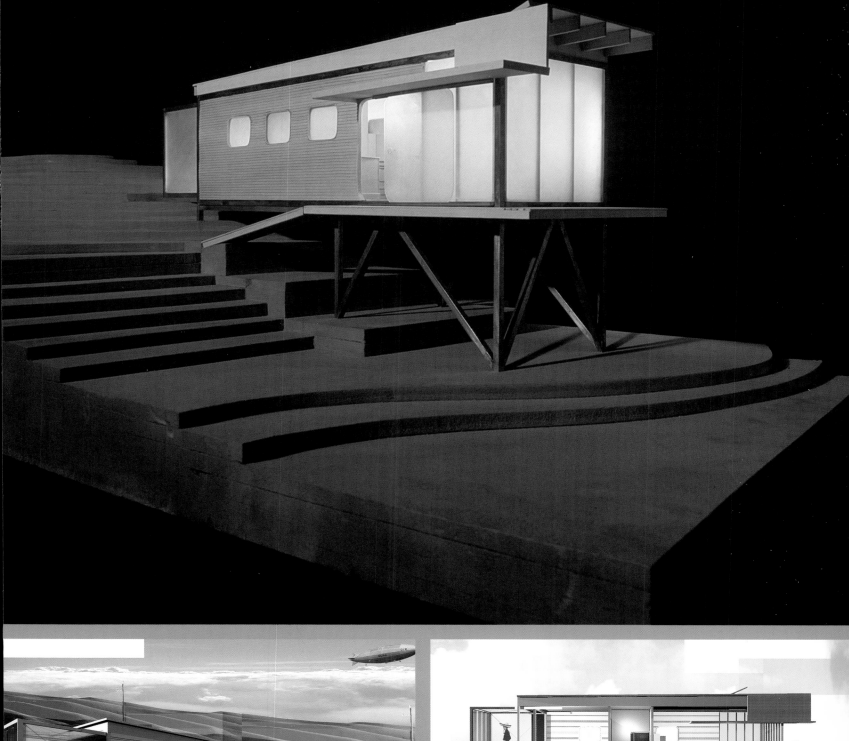

Established in 1992 in a suburb of Bombay, Dilip Chhabria's DC Design firm was set up to overcome some of the limitations imposed by mass production in the car manufacturing industry. The designer offers a bespoke service similar to that used in the early years of automobile production, when a customer could have a vehicle designed and built to suit his own needs and tastes. Chhabria employs a team of highly skilled artisans including panel beaters and painters who are able to produce exclusive cars and motor homes to order.

Exuba is a luxurious motor home built on the chassis of an Ashok Leyland Cargo truck. The interior is divided into a lounge area, chemical toilet, pantry, sleeping quarters, and a bar. However, the internal layout, color scheme and decoration, together with the external paintwork, can be fully personalized and arranged to suit the needs of the buyer. On-board amenities include a home entertainment system, air conditioning, personal computer, refrigerator, and microwave oven. The motor home's structure is provided by a tubular metal framework, which is sheathed in aluminum panels and then coated with a streamlined plastic finish. The interior is also sculpted in molded plastic, which has a textured finish and is decorated with wood laminate paneling. Other DC Design motor homes, such as the Lextran, which is based on a Mercedes Benz chassis, are produced using similar techniques and materials.

Movie stars who spend weeks at a time on location and business executives who need a workspace on wheels make up a large proportion of Chhabria's client base. The designer is a champion of individual expression in an industry dominated by generic styles and mass production. His top-quality vehicle conversions are popular with high-fliers who want to express a little of their own personality in their four-wheeled homes away from home.

Chhabria's top-flight motor homes are custom made according to his clients' needs. The contemporary styling and deluxe fittings have proved especially popular with India's movie stars who use the vehicles to provide a few home comforts while filming in remote locations.

Loft-living has shifted from a bohemian pursuit to the mainstream property market. Creating a home in a redundant warehouse was for a long time the preserve of eccentric artists, but has since mutated into a property developers' dream and contributed considerably to turning house buyers on to a different type of home. The M-House (pronounced "mouse") aims to do the same for trailer homes. It is a transportable dwelling that marries the up-market style of a smart loft apartment with the production and distribution process of the trailer home.

The portable house began life as a commission for a one-off prefabricated home to be located by the edge of a creek in Essex, southeast England. MAE, the architects behind the project, came up with a design for a house in two halves: one containing the lounge, kitchen, and dining area and one containing three bedrooms and two bathrooms. The two halves are designed to be transported separately and then fastened together on site. The idea was certainly not a new one. However, what distinguished it from other modular homes was the quality of its construction. The client, Tim Pyne, quickly recognized the potential for such a dwelling and developed it further with the architects for production on a commercial scale.

Although legally defined as a mobile home due to its size, the M-House complies with many of the strict building regulations applied to site-built houses. The walls are thoroughly insulated and structure is self-supporting so any interior partitions can be removed. Exterior finishes range from aluminum panels to cedar shingle and the timber-framed windows are quite unlike those usually seen on a trailer home.

M-House isn't revolutionary in terms of its technology but that was never the intention. "People are often suspicious of the new," says Michael Howe, the project architect. M-House is inspired by the traditional trailer home but brings to it the attention to detail and high specifications you'd expect to find in a well appointed apartment. Loft-living introduced a new language to domestic architecture and M-House takes that language to the trailer park.

In addition to providing homes on dry land the M-House may also be floated on a barge and the architects have developed a similar dwelling for use on roof tops. The open-plan interior, high-specification materials, and top of the range appliances give M-House the feel of an upmarket apartment, yet it is legally defined as a trailer home.

Tim Pyne and MAE Architects, UK
M-House, 2002

M-Pod for Living is a luxurious, dome-shaped dwelling designed as a self-contained holiday home for exotic, out-of-the-way locations. The stylish building is prefabricated as a kit of parts for shipping and then assembled at its chosen resting site. A base of either concrete slabs is used on flat land or steel frame for sloping sites. A one-bedroom M-Pod with an en-suite bathroom, living room, dining room, and kitchen with perimeter deck has a diameter of 12 meters. Several pods can be linked together to enlarge the living space or create a small cluster of dwellings.

The hemispherical roof is made from a modular system of ceramic tiles that clip into place over a framework of rolled steel beams. Photovoltaic cells are built into the roofing panels for solar energy collection as the dwelling needs to have the ability to generate its own power when positioned in remote places. The roof is also used to collect rainwater by channelling it into large gutters around the dwelling's perimeter and purifying it for reuse. A large curved window made from sliding glass panels opens up to the external deck and extends the available living space, while ornate sliding screens, carved from timber and covered with a fine bronze mesh are added to help keep insects at bay.

M-Pod's futuristic style gives it the look of a flying saucer. It rests lightly on the ground and the dome shape aids passive ventilation. The interior is compact but fabulously well-equipped. All the fixtures and fittings are of the highest quality and the contemporary look seems completely unrelated to a typical manufactured home. Blaess has adopted the prefabrication process and used it to create a stunning alternative to what typically springs to mind when we think of a mobile home.

The ornate timber screen provides a curtain around the internal areas of the house and is fitted with a bronze mesh to keep out insects.

Ronan and Erwan Bouroullec, France
Polystyrene House, 2003

Like La Petite Maison de Weekend (see p. 86), the Bouroullec brothers' Polystyrene House is a fusion of furniture design and architecture. The designers call it "micro architecture," flexible objects that sit somewhere between a room and a bed. An earlier example is the Lit Clos (2000), a small room for sleeping that is raised on steel legs and reached via a small ladder. Inspired by the small, closet-like beds that were once used in French farmhouses, the Lit Clos is a private chamber aimed at people who live and work in the same open-plan space.

The Bouroullec brothers demonstrated an attraction to polystyrene foam with the Brick shelving system (2001) designed for Cappellini. The material is light yet strong and incredibly versatile, but largely ignored by designers. Polystyrene House is a concept for a building constructed by slotting together sculpted blocks of foam. To make the house bigger you just add more pieces of foam. The individual sections are held in place by horizontal poles and the entire dwelling is sealed at each end by frames containing windows, a door and a chimney. Power cables and water pipes enter the dwelling through holes in these frames. The house is very functional but also humorous and packed with charm. Its shape and the technique used to construct it are perfectly suited to the polystyrene building blocks.

Polystyrene House takes the technology the designers used in Brick and develops it for use on a larger scale. The Polystyrene House maintains the distinctive clean and uncluttered form that characterizes the brothers' smaller works. Their approach is very different to that of an architect. Like Sam Buxton (see p. 78), they apply the knowledge and experience gained in product design to create bigger objects.

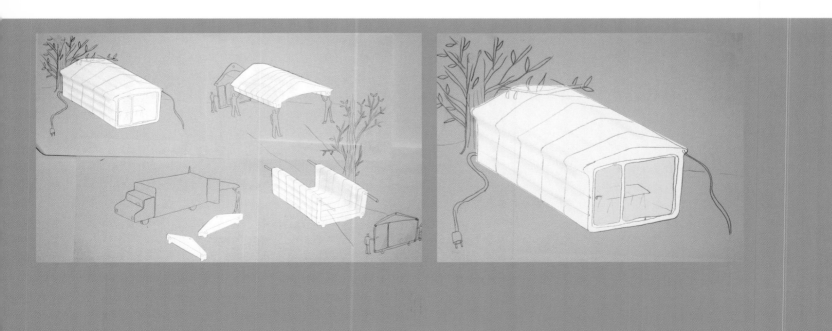

Better known for their innovative product designs, Ronan and Erwan Bouroullec's small house concept is constructed by slotting together precut blocks of polystyrene. Situated somewhere between a piece of furniture and a full-blown building, the designers describe such works as "micro architecture."

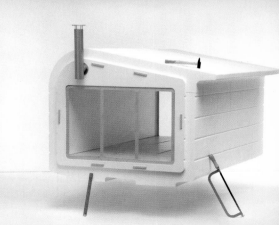

Andrew Winch Designs, UK
G-OBBJ, 2003

A private aircraft is perhaps the ultimate mobile home although very few are lived in for anything more than a brief stay. Most are used for charter by corporate clients and have the generic interior of a conference center. However, this design by Andrew Winch for Multiflight, a charter company based in northern England, is also designed to accommodate the company's owner and his family. The result is a combination of a corporate jet and a family home in the air.

Situated at the rear of the aircraft is the spacious master bedroom and master bathroom, the areas requiring the most privacy. Heading forward from here toward the cockpit the aircraft becomes less of a domestic space and more like an office. Subtle changes in seating patterns, decoration and lighting are employed by the designer to indicate the purpose of each section.

The aft lounge is an informal space separated from the master bedroom by a hallway, wardrobe and VIP bathroom. There is room to relax and the seating follows an informal arrangement suitable for dining or watching a movie. An arch divides the aft lounge from the forward lounge and conceals added storage space. The forward lounge is the place to do business. The seating is formally arranged to cater for ten people and the area is equipped with all the audio visual equipment needed for bombarding clients with extravagant presentations. This area is separated from the crew's quarters, galley, and cockpit by cupboards for briefcases, shoes, and coats.

The distinct layout of the aircraft's interior is very expressive of the manner in which we in the western world prefer to arrange our living spaces. Do-Ho Suh's *Seoul Home* (see p. 68) illustrates how, in the southeast Asian tradition, spaces are flexible and can be transformed for different uses. The western tradition is much more static and full of barriers that separate areas into designated functions. Space becomes a luxury when structured for a specific purpose, especially within the confines of an aircraft.

Softer colors and an informal seating pattern give the aft lounge a more relaxed mood to the forward lounge, which can be seen through the doorway in the background.

A queen-sized double bed is placed at an angle in the master bedroom to allow easy access from either side without needlessly taking up extra space. The bathroom has a limestone vanity unit, generous shower, and a toilet concealed beneath a leather bench.

Not strictly a mobile home, architect Peter Haimerl's Cocobello is a flexible unit suitable for a variety of applications. The neat capsule is aimed at artists and creative practitioners who don't necessarily want to be tied to a single location. It consists of three interlocked components that unfold using a pneumatic device to form a two-story studio. Sitting at the bottom is a concealed area designed to accommodate a small bathroom, kitchen, and storage space. The bright upper tier houses a spacious studio with large windows at either end, which can be rendered transparent or opaque depending on the intended use.

The internal structure is strong, light and manufactured from steel pipes. Plastic panels and carbon-fiber fabric are used for the external cladding, while the windows are plasticized glass and the interior walls are coated with compressed-reed paneling. Measuring only 3 × 6 × 3.5 meters when packed away, Cocobello can be moved from place to place without the need for a heavy goods vehicle, which substantially reduces the cost of transportation. There is no need to fit any external parts when unfolding the unit because it is completely self-contained. Essential elements, including the furniture, remain inside the box when it is packed for shipment.

Cocobello is activated by first sliding out the protruding sections that form the space of the upper half. Once these are in place a pneumatic lifting mechanism contained in the structure of the lower half elevates the upper tier into place. The T-formation of the unpacked studio provides a much greater floor space than its small footprint suggests. The shape is also very distinct, which makes the unit ideal for promotional purposes. Haimerl used it to display his Zoomtown project, a future vision of Europe's planning and infrastructure in which the Cocobello studios play an important role, at the 2003 architecture biennale in Rotterdam.

cocobello

A pneumatic lifting mechanism raises the upper part of the unit from its base. Cocobello is available with a range of finishes that make it ideal for use as a working promotional display case or exhibition space.

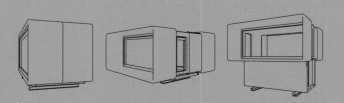

cocobello

Matias Creimer, Argentina
Dockable Dwelling, 2003

Creimer's Dockable Dwelling is a modular housing system concept that won the 2003 Home House Project organized by the Southeastern Center for Contemporary Art in California. His candy-colored proposal celebrates the endless possibilities offered by portable and prefabricated buildings.

Built along the lines of a factory-based modular system, the Dockable Dwelling incorporates a coupling system that allows each separate module to hook-up with another. Seven interconnecting modules make up the Dockable Dwelling system and include a terrace, kitchen, a living and dining area, a hallway and porch, a two bedroom unit, a master bedroom and bathroom unit, and a bedroom, laundry, and bathroom unit. Any configuration of the modules is possible and presents the opportunity to expand, contract and rearrange the home as new situations arise. The architect hopes that the transportability of the modules will encourage homeowners to sell on their unwanted units instead of destroying them; and when the piece reaches its life expectancy it will be recycled in the same way as automobiles.

Creimer's aim with the project is to make house construction much more efficient and therefore more cost-effective. He admits to being an admirer of the "hands on" craftsmanship of the building trades but believes on-site activity can eat up a large portion of the budget when it comes to building houses, money that can be better allocated to improving the quality and durability of the house. By splitting the home into interconnecting modules, Creimer has designed a system that can fully exploit assembly-line production and road-transport distribution. It also offers great flexibility to the homeowner who is able to choose the layout, fittings, and exterior color scheme of the home.

Unlike many recent examples of modular homes that attempt to imitate site-built houses, the Dockable Dwelling is proud to be mobile. The bright colors and playful shapes in Creimer's proposal make a stroll along the street seem like walking into a candy store.

The cocoon-shaped bedroom units are fitted with porthole windows that look like bug eyes and maintain privacy without blocking out too much natural light.

Matias Creimer, Argentina
Dockable Dwelling, 2003

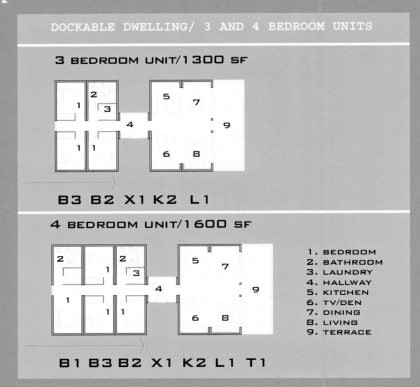

DOCKABLE DWELLING/ 3 AND 4 BEDROOM UNITS

3 BEDROOM UNIT/1300 SF

B3 B2 X1 K2 L1

4 BEDROOM UNIT/1600 SF

1. BEDROOM
2. BATHROOM
3. LAUNDRY
4. HALLWAY
5. KITCHEN
6. TV/DEN
7. DINING
8. LIVING
9. TERRACE

B1 B3 B2 X1 K2 L1 T1

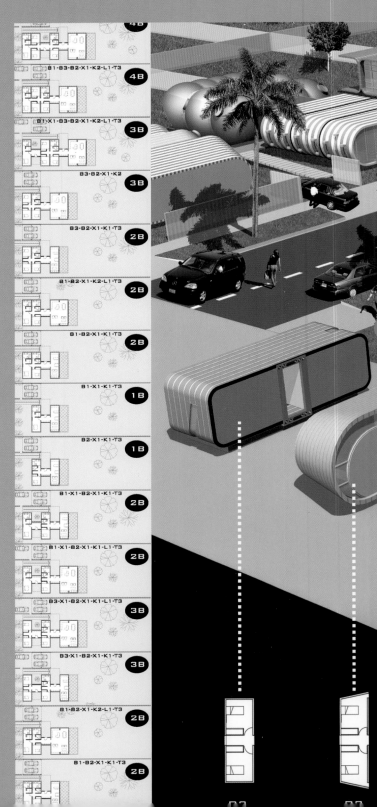

B1-B3-B2-X1-K2-L1-T3 — 4B

B1-X1-B3-B2-X1-K2-L1-T3 — 3B

B3-B2-X1-K2 — 3B

B3-B2-X1-K1-T3 — 2B

B1-B2-X1-K2-L1-T3 — 2B

B1-B2-X1-K1-T3 — 2B

B1-X1-K1-T3 — 1B

B2-X1-K1-T3 — 1B

B1-X1-B2-X1-K1-T3 — 2B

B1-X1-B2-X1-K1-L1-T3 — 2B

B3-X1-B2-X1-K1-L1-T3 — 3B

B3-X1-B2-X1-K1-T3 — 3B

B1-B2-X1-K2-L1-T3 — 2B

B1-B2-X1-K1-T3 — 2B

The seven modules pictured here include three different bedroom arrangements, a front porch and hallway, a kitchen and TV den, a combined lounge and dining area, and a sheltered terrace. Creimer's preference for bright colors and novel shapes cheers up the neighborhood, which seems a far cry from the typical image of a trailer park.

MD 144 is brutal in its honesty. Unlike many other prefab houses available in the USA it does not try to disguise itself as a regular site-built home. Indeed, MD 144 actually celebrates the inexpensive materials with which it is built.

Edgar Blazona is a self-taught furniture designer and he created MD 144 from a desire to create a multi-purpose dwelling with off-the-shelf materials such as fiberglass and corrugated steel. It looks raw and tough yet light enough to be kicked from place to place. Blazona used MD 144 as his accommodation at the Burning Man festival, which takes place in the August heat of the Nevada desert. The week-long event features all manner of portable dwellings, art works, music and performance. MD 144 performed well in the heat of the desert and its floor space was maximized by placing the bed on a mezzanine shelf.

MD 42 is a little more polished than its predecessor but was also used as an accommodation unit at Burning Man. Blazona collaborated on the dwelling with fellow designer Brice Gamble and like MD 144 it is also very easy to tear down and transport. Wood is the principle construction component and the interior is painted white, which helped to combat the hot desert sun. Glass replaces Lucite in the windows and the bed folds into the wall when not in use.

"The world is starving for architecture that is a little more approachable," says Blazona. "My work is accessible, it's in your face. I like to call it guerrilla architecture." Modular dwellings provide an ideal vehicle for Blazona and Gamble to communicate their ideas about architecture and design to a wider public. Because the buildings move they are able to interact with new audiences and new locations.

Measuring 3.66 x 3.66 x 3.66 meters, MD 144 is a flat-pack dwelling manufactured from galvanized steel, fiberglass, Lucite and Plexiglas panels, corrugated metal, and veneered MDF flooring. Pictured at the 2001 Burning Man Festival, Black Rock City, Nevada, the unit was Biozone's accommodation during the event. The ladder gives access to the sleeping loft, which is raised to free up the floor space.

MD 42 is slightly smaller than MD 144 at 1.83 x 2.13 x 2.44 meters, but it is made with much higher specification materials. The bed is a canvas cradle that folds away when not in use, maple ply is used for the floor and ceiling, and the walls are custom made with wooden siding, which doesn't require a structural framework for support.

Otto Steidle, Germany
Nomad's Tower, 2000

Created by architect Otto Steidle for the Biennale de Venezia, 2000, Nomad's Tower is a fusion of two ideas representing two very different societies. On the one hand it is a tower, a monument associated for thousands of years with settled civilizations. And on the other it's a mobile dwelling, the home of the nomad. The two cultures are often in conflict with each other but on the back of the architect's Unimog truck they are united as one. The piece is full of similar contradictions, and films and images relating to the various themes it throws up are displayed on monitors around the tower.

A metal frame provides the tower's structure and this is coated in a wooden skin with shutters that open to reveal a sleeping cabin and a number of television sets. Steidle is not only the architect of the project but also its builder and driver. In a trip lasting 26 days Steidle drove the Nomad's Tower from Germany to Venice, the city where it was finally exhibited. He sees the Nomad's Tower as a combination of home, work place, and tool. The piece raises many questions about how we live now and how we might survive in the future.

The Nomad's Tower's unusual form and its bright color scheme inspire the curiosity of passers, resulting in the breakdown of certain social barriers. It is a beacon that engages people and instigates discussion. While stopping off in a town or village the vehicle interrupts day-to-day routines and brings with it a festive spirit. Through this disruption the Nomad's Tower has the potential to make people see their surroundings in an altogether different way. The mood of a place is altered, normality and conventions defied.

Nomad's Tower seen here (right) at the 2000 Venice Biennale, and (left) on a tour of German cities.

Brigata Tognazzi (Walter A. Aprile, Italy; Anna Barbara, Italy; Rachaporn Choochuey, Thailand; Stefano Mirti, Italy; Akihiro Otsuka, Japan; Luca Poncellini, Italy; Andrea Volpe, Italy)
Polycarbonate House, 2000

122

It is not easy to accommodate many guests when you live in a small apartment in Tokyo. This was the dilemma faced by Stefano Mirti when three of his friends from back home in Italy decided to pay him a visit. There was no way they could afford a hotel for the three-week stay, and there were no campsites located nearby. Being architects, Mirti and his friends in Tokyo devised a plan to build a temporary house for the visitors. Luckily, the idea coincided with the Mukojima arts and architecture festival where they were offered space to build it.

The house, built entirely from polycarbonate sheeting, was inspired by the neat little shelters built by some of Tokyo's homeless community. It took a great deal of planning before the house was actually built. The friends in Italy worked on prototype models and the friends in Tokyo did all the necessary negotiating to obtain permission for the build and sponsorship to help cover the cost of materials. On arrival in Tokyo the two groups teamed up to build the temporary house, which took one week to complete. The construction process evolved into an event for the local community and people kindly donated stones to make a patio and flowers and candles for decoration. A neighbor offered to connect the house to his own water and electricity services while others maintained a generous supply of sweet green tea.

The finished house covered a floor space of 16 square meters and included a small kitchen, shower, toilet, living room, patio, and sleeping area. The foundation was made with concrete slabs and the walls were attached to a wooden frame positioned around it. No structural framework was required because the polycarbonate sheets are self-supporting. However, further insulation of the sheets was required around the sleeping area to keep it cool in the hot weather. The three visitors lived in the house for the rest of their stay. On the final day it was dismantled in a matter of hours and packed away to be used again sometime.

Living in a small apartment presents a real problem when friends want to stay. One possible solution is to build a temporary dwelling such as Brigata Tognazzi's Polycarbonate House. The narrow house measures 2 x 8 x 2 meters and is easy to erect and dismantle.

It was first built during the Mukojima festival in Kyojima, Sumida-ku, Tokyo, May 2000 and neighbors kindly connected it to their own electricity and water supplies for the duration of the event.

PolycarbonateHouse

ポリカーボネイトの家 東京向島 平成12年6月

Andrew Winch Designs, UK

Alithia, 2002
White Rabbit, 1994

Yachts don't suffer the same image problems as land-bound mobile homes. Even the most dilapidated home on water maintains a certain grace and allure that even top-of-the-range homes on wheels fail to capture. A marina mirrors the idea of the plug-in city that was popular with architects in the 1960s: yachts are like portable living pods while harbors provide the infrastructure for docking. A constant flow of arrivals and departures alters the dynamics of the floating community but the physical framework remains essentially the same.

White Rabbit and Alithia are two very different types of yacht but both are fabulously luxuriant. The largest and most ornate is White Rabbit, a 50-meter motor-powered yacht named and themed after its owner's lucky birth sign. The spectacular interior is centered on a dramatic triple-deck atrium. At the top is a huge lounge area that transforms from a state-of-the-art conference facility to a casino complete with full-sized roulette table and slot machines. A circle of white silk sofas and a Steinway Grand piano are the focal points of the main saloon, and in the dining room the twelve place-settings are marked by Chinese zodiac signs on the ceiling above. The huge private yacht is capable of accommodating up to twenty guests in statesman-like comfort and has a range of around 4,000 miles.

Alithia is a sailing yacht designed for speed and the minimal style of its interior echoes the sleek exterior profile. Measuring 40 meters Alithia is much smaller than White Rabbit and has a radically different interior. The owners and their family of five children wanted a racing yacht that would also serve as a family home for a two-year-long sailing trip around the world. The result is an informal, elegant and uncluttered design with none of the extravagance of White Rabbit.

The opulent gaming area in White Rabbit's upper lounge, which doubles up as a high-tech conference center during working hours, is fitted with slot machines, video arcade games, and a full size roulette table. The ceiling is adorned with lucky white rabbits and contrasts sharply with the restrained interior of Alithia. Canadian maple is used throughout this sleek sailing yacht and natural light floods into the lower salon through the striking wrap-around windscreen.

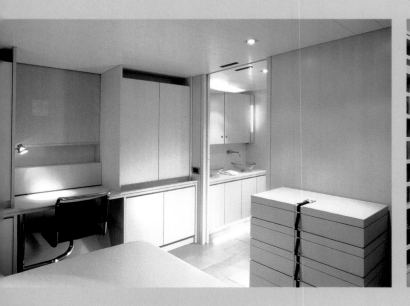

It may not be the prettiest mobile home on the road, but Sunflower is an incredibly sophisticated piece of machinery. The engine is not fuelled by diesel or gas but SVO—Straight Vegetable Oil. Instead of filling up at the gas station, James Haldane refuels at fast food outlets on dumpster grease. The waste vegetable oil is filtered and powers his engine just like diesel, but without the pollution. It is a surprisingly efficient alternative to diesel and is available at a fraction of the cost.

Haldane, an audiovisual technician, has lived on board Sunflower for nine years. His home enables him to drastically reduce his living expenses and his impact on the environment. He designed the vehicle to be as big as possible while still able to fit in a parking space. The compact interior provides enough space for a double bed, dining table, a gas-powered oven and hob, kitchen sink, refrigerator, and plenty of cupboards. Skylights on the roof flood the interior with natural light while energy-efficient white LEDs provide illumination at night.

Haldane lives in the van full-time and together with people such as A. R. Thomson (see p. 42) is part of a substantial network of eco-RV enthusiasts. This mobile community provides a forum to exchange information and advice relating to the low-impact lifestyle its members advocate. The sense of community is one of the most appealing attributes of the eco-RV network. The individual mobile homes may be self-sufficient, but van living would be a far more arduous prospect without the informal society that has evolved around it.

Even the most minute savings in energy consumption provide a source of fascination for the dedicated eco-RV buff. Energy efficiency is the driving force behind homes such as Sunflower, but it not only saves power it generates it, too. Mounted on its roof is an 800 watt system of solar modules. These charge a battery bank which is inverted to 120 Volts AC to run household appliances and enough electricity to power sound stages and festival concerts in remote locations.

As its name suggests, Sunflower is powered by a combination of solar energy and waste vegetable oil from deep-fat fryers. Since Sunflower is a very small dwelling Haldane could afford to use top quality building materials such as solid maple for the kitchen counter.

The elaborate Dekotora Vans are a far cry from the functionality of eco-RVs such as Sunflower (see p. 126), but what they have in common is a community of involved enthusiasts bonded by a shared passion for life on wheels. Where appearances aren't so important to the eco-RV network they are everything to the young van devotees of Japan. With high specification interiors and immaculate finishings, there is more than a hint of the opulence of White Rabbit (see p. 124) about these extraordinary machines.

Japan's custom van scene has its roots in the USA where the trend grew from the late 1940s and reached its high point in the 1970s. Customized vans came to represent a new and free lifestyle for young people who were eager to escape the family home, but lacked the finances, or the desire and probably the permission to leave it completely. B-movies and magazines helped propel the scene into the international arena and sparked a trend for vannin' on the other side of the Pacific.

In Japan, the Toyota Hiace is the preferred vehicle for customization. Accessories such as tail fins, spoilers, and wheel trims are all employed to alter the physical shape of the van. The transformations can be astounding, with slick paintwork, airbrushed illustrations and mesmerizing illumination all adding to the overall effect. The expressive, futuristic styling mixes up influences from arcade games to sci-fi comics. The interiors are even more impressive and demonstrate meticulous attention to detail. Some contain elaborate arrangements of very loud speakers that take up all the inside space. Others are fitted with a bed or sofa and are decked out in a style that wouldn't look out of place in a themed love hotel. And like a love hotel, the vans provide an intimate and private space away from the family home.

The time and effort invested while customizing these remarkable vehicles is astounding. Fantasy is a major influence in many of the designs. Some vans look as if they have driven straight out of an arcade game, others are elaborately painted with pop stars, and further examples are decorated with scenes from manga comics. Interiors are equally unrestrained and carry the fantasy even further.

The tradition for decorating vehicles is deeply embedded in the territory that modern-day Pakistan covers. Before the advent of motor-driven transport freight carriers beautified their boats, animal-drawn wagons, and livestock with ornate carvings and murals similar to those now applied to trucks. Since Pakistan was created in 1947 there has been a dramatic increase in the variety of elaborate decorative styles. Different patterns and motifs have evolved in different regions of the country so it is possible to know immediately where a particular truck hails from. Symbols representing peacock feathers are typical of the Punjab and Sindh, whereas carved wooden doors are associated with Swat and Peshawar. No matter which part of Pakistan the truck originates from it will always carry some sort of protection against the "evil eye." This can be in the form of large painted eyes, black scarves, or an old shoe hanging from its bumper. Interior decoration is just as elaborate as that on the outside. Mirrors, beads, and fine cushions give the cabin opulent feel while many trucks are also equipped with powerful sound systems.

The core of the truck-decorating industry is located in Karachi, Pakistan's thriving port city. Drivers flock there from all over the region to pick up goods from cargo ships. The city is home to many skilled craftsmen familiar with the wide variety of regional styles. There is a competitive spirit among the truck drivers who try to outdo each other with the most striking designs. Jamil-ud-Din and Haider Ali, the men responsible for the Smithsonian Institute's 1976 Bedford, were singled out from Karachi's artisans because of their great versatility. The pair was invited to Washington DC to take part in the 2002 Smithsonian Folklife Festival, which had the Silk Road as its theme. Din and Ali fused a variety of styles to give visitors to the festival a comprehensive introduction to their art. The painted murals show scenes from all over Pakistan, and these are presented side-by-side with images of Washington DC itself.

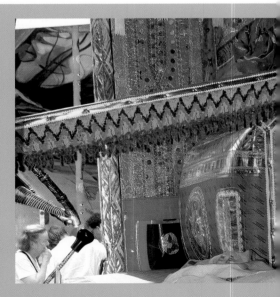

Jamil-ud-Din and Haider Ali were invited as masters of their craft to participate in the 2002 Smithsonian Folklife Festival, which had the Silk Road as its theme. Din took care of the bodywork and Ali the painting. They decorated the 1976 Bedford truck with shapes, emblems, and patterns used in the different regions of Pakistan while also including images from their first trip to the USA.

Weighing just over 260 kilograms when fully loaded, Behemoth maybe a heavyweight bruiser of a bicycle but it barely makes flyweight when compared to other mobile homes. Its predecessors Winnebiko I and II are even lighter, and with the three machines Steven Roberts pedaled over 27,000 kilometers around the USA. Unlike the majority of projects in this book, Roberts's array of high-tech homes on wheels are not formed by a need for movable shelter but by a passion for communication.

The adventure started in 1983 when Roberts incorporated his interests in cycling, electronics, adventure, and ham radio into a pioneering mobile-home concept. He ditched his suburban lifestyle and took to the road on a recumbent bicycle dubbed Winnebiko. A portable computer, a six-watt solar panel, and the data communication link CompuServe gave Roberts the freedom to cycle around the United States while making a living from magazine assignments, consultant positions, and other freelance activity. Winnebiko came to represent a new type of freedom. Roberts described it as "a machine that eloquently symbolized the daring notion that people could indeed be free, follow their dreams, and break the chains that had always bound them to their desks."

In 1986 Winnebiko was replaced by the much more sophisticated Winnebiko II, which satisfied Roberts's main objective of wanting to be able to type while pedaling. Packed with switches, processors, and LEDs the machine carried Roberts a further 9,500 kilometers. His physical location grew less and less important. What mattered most was maintaining a presence in the online networks. "Home, quite literally," says Roberts, "became an abstract electronic concept."

Behemoth [Big Electronic Human-Energized Machine … Only Too Heavy], the final incarnation of Roberts's wired bicycles, was three and a half years in development, but he only used it for a further 1,500 kilometers. In addition to the computing facilities of a small laboratory, the bike and its trailer also carries a full suite of camping and life-support equipment. The road no longer held so many surprises for Roberts and in 1992 he switched his attention to water transport with the Microship project.

Behemoth is the result of a three-and-a-half-year development program. It carries a full suite of camping and life-support equipment including medical supplies, food rations, water filters, emergency flares, cooking and washing facilities, clothing, a tent, and more. There's a whole array of electronic gadgetry and the bike itself has 105 speeds.

Steve Roberts
Winnebiko I, 1983
Winnebiko II, 1986

Winnebiko I was the first and least sophisticated of Roberts's three bicycles, but it was equipped with all the essentials Roberts's needed to break free from his desk and embark on an adventure with staggering implications. Way back in 1983 it was obvious to Roberts that the emerging data communication networks were making his physical location less and less significant.

Winnebiko II appeared in 1986 and enabled Roberts to type while cycling. It was equipped with a speech synthesizer, a 20 watt solar panel, and a data communication system for email via ham radio.

Decorated with murals that celebrate the Harley Davison motorcycle, Live to Ride / Ride to Live is not just a show truck but a hard-working haulage vehicle. Much of its time is spent on the long drive between Michigan and California transporting goods such as furniture on the route south and fresh produce on the way home. It was customized by its drivers, Vetta Todd and John Noakes, and is part of a large fleet owned by Ever Fresh Transportation. Todd and Noakes are well-established on the US show truck scene and Live to Ride / Ride to Live has won them many trophies at competitive events such as the Trucker's Jamboree in Reno, Nevada. Vetta Todd has since customized an additional truck named 9–11 as a tribute to those who died in the September 11 terrorist attack on the World Trade Center.

Live to Ride/Ride to Live has a mural painted on either side of its sleeper by Scott Signs of Michigan. Both depict a highway winding its way through mountainous countryside. One side has an illustration of the scene at sunset and the other at sunrise. A motorcyclist is pictured cruising along the roads on a Harley Davison and following him is a classic Peterbilt truck. Both scenes celebrate freedom and capture some of the romance of the open road. Ever Fresh own the truck and pay for many of the improvements. However the drivers also invest a great deal of their own money and massive amounts of time in maintaining their vehicle to such a high standard. Ever Fresh has three customized trucks in its fleet and all provide excellent PR for the firm.

Preparing a truck for competition means plenty of hard work. Minute details make all the difference when it comes down to picking the winners at such contests. Everything—including the undercarriage and engine— has to be in immaculate condition. Even the tires are polished and every letter around the rim is colored to complement the paintwork of the truck's body. The pride the drivers show in their truck goes down well with its owners and the customers, who are regularly blown away by its exceptional appearance.

Live to Ride / Ride to Live is a Peterbilt 379 customized by the drivers Vetta Todd and John Noakes. Murals were painted by Scott Signs, Michigan and the interior fit out was performed by Eagle Interior Concepts, Oklahoma. The truck is owned by Carl Bossenbrock and Mont Reed of Ever Fresh Transportation, Michigan.

A conventional RV was nowhere near sufficient for photographer Rob Gray's retirement plans so he decided to design and build his own. Measuring over 10 meters in length Wothahelizat is a giant among motor homes and was built on the chassis of a fire truck. This rugged foundation has given the vehicle extraordinary off-road capabilities, which means it can be driven across terrain that would destroy any regular motor home. Wothahelizat also has enough storage capacity to endure lengthy stays in Australia's remote outback without having stock up on supplies every two or three days. "If you are going to spend time and effort getting to a remote spot," asserts Gray, "it doesn't make sense to stay for only a day or two." To overcome this he has built a monster that can carry ample supplies to live comfortably in the bush for around a month.

In driving mode the motor home resembles a tough metal box on wheels. The roof is stepped at the rear to allow for extra storage space under the floor and a viewing deck folds down to form an extension to the lounge area. Sleeping quarters are positioned above the driver's cabin and the roof here pops up to provide greater headroom. In addition to the lounge and bedroom there is a kitchen, bathroom, toilet, and masses of extra storage space. Wothahelizat is not just a home for Gray but also a working environment and so requires plenty of power, which is supplied through a combination of batteries, a generator, and solar cells.

Gray is part of a growing community in Australia of retired people who spend pretty much all of their time on the road. He embodies the spirit of innovation that spawned the whole RV phenomenon. Wothahelizat functions as a full-time home and office and provides access to areas that other motor homes just cannot reach.

This extraordinary motor home was built by photographer Rob Gray on the chassis of a fire truck. He designed it with three specific criteria in mind. Firstly, it provides a comfortable live/work space that can be occupied for long periods of time. Second, it has excellent off-road capabilities for travel in Australia's remote outback. And finally, it has enough storage space for supplies to sustain comfortable living in out of the way locations for weeks at a time.

Rob Gray, Australia
Wothahelizat, 2001

Wothahelizat is coated with metal panels that are closed in transit but open up when stationary to form a spectacular viewing deck and reveal enormous windows around a raised lounge area.

Albrecht, Donald and Elizabeth Johnson. *New Hotels for Global Nomads*. London / New York: Merrell Publishers in association with Cooper-Hewitt, National Design Museum, 2002.

Ascherson, Neal. *Black Sea*. London: Jonathan Cape, 1995.

Atkinson, Rebecca. "The Green Machine" in *This Magazine*. Toronto, August 2002.

Braithwaite, David. *Fairground Architecture*. London: H. Evelyn, 1968.

Corrin, Lisa G. *Do-Ho Suh*. London: Serpentine Gallery and Seattle Art Museum, Seattle, 2002.

Falzon, Laurence. "Hans-Walter Müller's air castles" in *Air-Air: Celebrating Inflatables*. Monaco: Le 27e Stratagème, Inflate Unit Research and Grimaldi Forum, 2001.

Fuksas, Massimiliano and Doriana O. Madrelli. *Città: Less Aesthetics More Ethics*. Venice / New York: Marsilio and Rizzoli International Publications, 2000.

Gallanti, Fabrizio. "Emergency Modules, Chile" in *Abitare*, issue 421, Milan, October 2002.

Garber, Bette S. *Custom Semi Trucks*. St. Paul, Minnesota: Motorbooks International, 2003.

Johns, Peter. "Radar Shelter" in Architecture Australia, www.architectureaustralia.com.au/aa/aaprintissue.php?issueid=200207&article=3. July 2002.

Jones, Uma. "Van Goth" in *Intersection Magazine*, issue 4, London, 2003.

Kronenburg, Robert. *Portable Architecture*. Oxford: Architectural Press, 2000 (second edition).

Lovegrove, Keith. *Airline: Identity, Design and Culture*. New York, TeNeues, 2000.

Matthias, Ludwig. *Mobile Architektur*. Stuttgart: Deutsche Verlags-Anstalt, 1998.

Middendorp, Chris. "There's nothing like a crazy idea…" in *The Age*, www.theage.com.au/articles/2002/05/28/1022569769448.html. May 28, 2002.

Molho, Renata. "Transformables" in *Abitare*, issue 405, Milan, April 2001.

"No Guts, No Glory." *The Age*: www.theage.com.au/cgibin/ common/popupPrintArticle.pl?path=/articles/2003/09/23 /1064082997618.html. September 24, 2003.

Oliver, Paul. *African Shelter*. London: Arts Council of Great Britain, 1975.

Oliver, Paul. *Dwellings*. London: Phaidon, 2003.

Oliver, Paul. *Encyclopedia of Vernacular Architecture of the World*, vols. I and II. Cambridge: Cambridge University Press, 1997.

Pearson, David. *Freewheeling Homes*. London: Gaia Books Limited, 2002.

Perry, Paul and Ken Babbs. *On the Bus: the complete guide to the legendary trip of Ken Kesey and the Merry Pranksters and the birth of the counterculture*. London: Plexus Publishing Limited, 1990.

Pinto, Roberto. *Lucy Orta*. London: Phaidon, 2003.

Restany, Pierre and Lucy Orta. *Process of Transformation*. Paris: Jean-Michel Place, 1998.

Saup, Michael. "The Myth of Omnipresence—Nomadic Lies" in *Art India*, vol. 7, issue 4, quarter 4, 2002.

Siegal, Jennifer. *Mobile: The Art of Portable Architecture*. Princeton: Princeton Architectural Press, 2002.

"Strategies of Urban Appropriation." *Abitare*, issue 423, Milan, December 2002.

Tsuzuki, Kyoichi. *Traffic Art*. Kyoto: Kyoto Shoin, 1990.

Weir, Shelagh. *The Bedouin: Aspects of the Material Culture of the Bedouin of Jordan: World of Islam Festival 1976*. London: World of Islam Festival Publishing Company Ltd., 1976.

Williams, Gareth. *Matali Crasset*. Paris: Pyramyd NTCV, 2003.

Wilson, Nerissa. *Gypsies and Gentlemen: The Life and Times of the Leisure Caravan*. London: Columbus Books, 1986.